CROSSING THE BORDER

CROSSING THE BORDER

An Expositional Study of Colossians

by

GUY H. KING

CHRISTIAN LITERATURE CRUSADE
Fort Washington, Pennsylvania 19034

CHRISTIAN LITERATURE CRUSADE
Fort Washington, Pennsylvania 19034

CANADA
Box 189, Elgin, Ontario K0G 1E0

Fourth Impression 1969
First American Edition 1974

*This edition published under special
arrangement with*

Marshall, Morgan & Scott, Ltd.
116 Baker Street
London, W1M 2BB, England

SBN 87508-274-2

DEDICATION

This is my last book written from
Christ Church, Beckenham.

I therefore send it forth

IN MEMORY OF
And
IN GRATITUDE FOR

The uncountable, & unaccountable kindnesses
of that grand congregation.

Canon Guy H. King completed the manuscript of this book September 28th 1956. He preached his last sermon September 30th 1956, taking as his text Numbers xiii. 23–33 with the keynote of "Crossing the Border into the Promised Land of God's best"—emphasizing the theme of *Full Salvation*. This theme also runs through this book as its main thought; hence its title "Crossing the Border". The dedication was written after the author's retirement from Christ Church, Beckenham, had been announced. He passed to his rest October 1st 1956, and it is thought that many who have found his books a source of inspiration and guidance in Bible study would like to have the notes of his last sermon, which are reproduced on the following page.

THE PUBLISHERS.

GRAPES, GIANTS, AND GRASSHOPPERS
Numbers xiii. 23–33.

These three words sum up The Majority Report of a Commission of Enquiry sent to assess the situation, and to present a report.

Moses, borders, Promised Land; I, borders, Christian life, land, promises.

Decision: enter, or remain outside?

THE GRAPES of Incomparable Blessing.

Never such grapes; never such blessings.
Pardon of sins—Isaiah i. 18.
Peace of mind—Philippians iv. 7.
Power for victory—1 John v. 4.
Prospect of Heaven—John xiv. 2.
Pilot on the voyage—Psalm xciii. 4.
Pleasures of GOD—Psalm xvi. 11.
Purpose in life—Acts xxvii. 23.
Pictures of consistency—Hebrews xiii. 7.
Presence of CHRIST—Hebrews xiii. 5.
No wonder, Psalm xxxiv. 8; Proverbs iv. 18.

THE GIANTS of Immense Opposition.

Attracted by, grapes; no use, giants!
Giant Difficult—never be able to keep it up.
Giant Doubt—can't be sure.
Giant Dismal—"giving up".
Giant Delay—later on means never.

THE GRASSHOPPERS of Inadequate Self.

In own sight—in their sight.
That was the end of the Majority Report; but Minority.

THE GOD OF INVINCIBLE POWER.

Able to save—able to keep.
It is not we, but He.
Over the border, then, into the Promised Land of GOD's best.
"I've never let one go yet."

FOREWORD

We shall not have gone far in our reading of Colossians before we call to mind some remarks of Peter concerning "our beloved brother Paul", in whose Epistles, he says, "are some things hard to be understood". In this particular letter there are certainly some very difficult passages. I have, in this Study, tried not to by-pass these perplexities, but have offered, with all deference, my own thoughts about them.—Difficulties, yes; but what Delights are here, too. I can only prayerfully hope that my clumsy efforts at exposition will not have spoiled too much the glories and beauties of this Divinely inspired Scripture.

Christ Church Vicarage,   G.H.K.
Beckenham.

CONTENTS

HIS TACTFUL APPROACH

Tactful Approach

1 Paul, an apostle of Jesus Christ by the will of God, and Timotheus *our* brother,

2 To the saints and faithful brethren in Christ which are at Colossè: Grace *be* unto you, and peace, from God our Father and the Lord Jesus Christ.

HIS TACTFUL APPROACH

I. 1–2

MANY writers have adopted the form of letters to express themselves—among the ancients there was Cicero, at a later time there was Erasmus, and coming on there were Thomas Gray, Horace Walpole, William Cowper, Charles Lamb and Sir Walter Scott; and there was Samuel Rutherford, who wrote his from prison; and right down to C. S. Lewis' *Screwtape Letters*—and so many others in between.

This ministry of letter writing was much used in the Early Church, and, as we know, the New Testament contains no less than twenty of them—we feel that Hebrews is more of a treatise than a letter. More than half of these letters were written by Paul. We speak humanly, for we do not forget that behind him is the inspiring HOLY SPIRIT—"words . . . which the HOLY GHOST teacheth", as he says in 1 Corinthians ii. 13. Isn't it interesting that GOD uses this method, as so many other methods, to convey His truth to human minds? I sometimes wonder why it is not employed more by Christian people, especially by shy folk who find it so difficult to speak about the things of GOD, but who could, perhaps, by prayerful tact write to another about things that matter most—perchance a simple testimony to what the Saviour means to the writer, and what He could, and would, mean to the reader. Who shall measure what such a ministry might accomplish in His Name.

Well now, here is the great apostle engaged upon his correspondence. Can you not almost hear him as he dictates sentence by sentence—some of the sentences, by the way, so long that, as in Ephesians, the full stops are almost a rarity. He certainly did dictate his letters, as, for instance, we observe in Romans xvi. 22, "I, Tertius, who wrote this epistle". I wonder what the Roman guard thought as he listened to the inspired words—perhaps these very words were part of the means whereby Paul was able to lead some of the soldiers "that kept him", Acts xxviii. 16, to CHRIST, these "saints in Cæsar's household", as Philippians iv. 22 describes them.

Though the letters were dictated, it seems that, in concluding, the apostle would take the pen in his own hand, and write a few words of personal salutation. "The salutation of Paul with mine own hand, which is the token in every epistle: so I write", 2 Thessalonians iii. 17; 1 Corinthians xvi. 21. How pathetically he remarks, "See what big letters I make when I write you in my own hand", Galatians vi. 11, Moffatt—was that because of bad eyesight, which some think was his "thorn in the flesh", 2 Corinthians xii. 7? And what about that other poignant reference at the end of this very Epistle that we are to study together, "The salutation by the hand of me, Paul. Remember my bonds", Colossians iv. 18? Why that last phrase? Was it just that he begged them to remember before GOD his irksome captivity? I think not. Bear in mind that he is bound at the wrist to a Roman soldier, and so he makes but a poor fist at his handwriting. I suggest that he offers this as an excuse for his perhaps illegible signature. Thus, then, we overhear him dictating to his amanuensis. Did Tychicus take it down in shorthand? A form of shorthand was practised among the Greeks, before CHRIST, and among the Latins of Cicero's day, 60 B.C. Sir Isaac Pitman was not the inventor of the art, though the introducer of a most useful method.

But now, the missive has reached its destination, and on one Lord's Day, as the church at Colossæ is assembled for worship, someone rises, and announces, "We have a letter from our beloved brother Paul". Would that not create an excited stir? It is thought that Paul was not the human founder of this church, writing as he was to these

"many as have not seen my face in the flesh", Colossians
ii. 1, but it is evident that he was well-known to them, and
highly esteemed among them. Indeed, Epaphras, the
reputed founder, Colossians i. 7, was at the very time of
Paul's writing at Rome, Colossians iv. 12–13, seemingly to
consult the apostle concerning certain false teaching that
was being promulgated among the church members. This
heresy is dealt with at large in the course of the Epistle.
In fact, we may say that the theme of the Epistle is "The
Church". Dr. Graham Scroggie adds that the keyword is
"Fulness"—all that the Church needs is in CHRIST. And
I see that Dr. Campbell Morgan divides up the main part
of the Epistle into (a) The Glorious CHRIST and His
Church: Provision, and (b) The Church and her glorious
CHRIST: Possession. Be it so; and for ourselves, we proceed to our more detailed examination of the letter, which
we might think of as an essay in Learning by Correspon-
dence, and we begin with Paul's lesson in tactful approach.

THE SUBTLE REFERENCE TO HIS AUTHORITY

He doesn't throw his weight about, as he was so well
entitled to do; but he just throws in, almost casually, the
fact that he is "*an apostle*", as if to remind his hearers that,
in what he has to say, he speaks with all the authority
that his important position gives him.

But does he legitimately belong to "this apostleship",
Acts i. 25? Some people consider that Peter proceeded
precipitously in moving to the election of Matthias in the
place of Judas. They advance the argument that to settle
the matter by "lot" was wrong, seeing that in the Christian
age the HOLY SPIRIT should have been their guide. But
we remember that He had not yet been given to the Church
at Pentecost; and, in any case, He was as able to lead by
lot as He had done in past ages in "the whole disposing
thereof is of the Lord", Proverbs xvi. 33. Another objec-
tion is that Matthias is never heard of again; but is

Lebbæus, or Simon Zelotes? Anyhow, the suggestion that Peter made a mistake is evidently not shared by the Early Church herself, since the number of the apostolate seems to have been officially regarded as complete again after the election of Matthias—see Acts vi. 2, "Then *the twelve* called the multitude of the disciples unto them". Of course, if Paul had been intended to become a member of the original band, there was another vacancy on the death of James, Acts xii. 2; but in reality he does not appear to have been eligible for the post, inasmuch as he did not fulfil the conditions, "men which have companied with us all the time that the Lord JESUS went in and out among us", Acts i. 21.

It is interesting to recall that Barnabas is linked with Paul as an apostle, in Acts xiv. 14. Notwithstanding all that has been said, there is no doubt, or question, of the reality and authority of Paul's apostleship. In the controversial Epistle to the Galatians he finds it incumbent to state the fact of his position, for he is to deal weighty blows on behalf of the truth. So he declares himself as "an apostle, not of men, neither by man, but by JESUS CHRIST, and GOD the Father", Galatians i. 1. Not that he boasted of the privilege, but ever held it in deepest humility, and profoundest gratitude, "as one born out of due time, for I am the least of the apostles, that am not meet to be called an apostle. . . ." 1 Corinthians xv. 8–9. Great men are, at heart, humble men; and true humility is of great value in the sight of GOD. Says 1 Peter v. 5, "Be clothed with humility, for GOD giveth grace to the humble". The thought of Paul's innate humility in the face of his high office leads one to think that perhaps there is no limit to what GOD can do with us if only we are humble enough! Many Christian careers have served to underline that feeling. When, in Romans xi. 13, Paul speaks of himself as "the apostle of the Gentiles", he adds, "I magnify mine office", but he doesn't magnify himself. Well—Paul makes here but gentle use of his claim to be an apostle. It is part of his tactful approach to his readers. And here is a further instance of the same—

THE DELICATE ALLUSION TO HIS READERS

He calls them "saints", 2. The word in itself has no moral or ethical connotation, but simply means, set apart. We speak of a church as a holy place—not that there is anything special about its brick and stone and wood, except that it is set apart for the worship of GOD. We speak of the Bible as a holy book—not that there is anything particular about its pages or binding, except that it is set apart for the conveyance to man of the inspired message of GOD. We speak of the sacramental element as holy bread—not that it is in any sense different from ordinary bread, except that it is set apart at the service to be a reminder to us of the broken body of the crucified Son of GOD. In just that sense the Christian becomes, as it were automatically, a saint, a holy person—he is set apart from the company of ordinary people, set apart for GOD. Only, unlike our illustrative objects mentioned above, he is a sentient being, a personality. They can only be holy in use, and can never be changed in themselves; but he can proceed from being merely holy in position to being holy in condition. That is, of course, the justification of the translators of the Authorised Version when, in Romans i. 7, and in 1 Corinthians i. 2, they add two little words that are not in the Greek, but which they infer to be the intention of the apostle. They render the phrase, not "called saints"—which, as we have seen, is an accurate statement of the fact—but, "called *to be* saints". In other words, we are called to be what we are. A soldier must, by his bearing and behaviour, live up to his profession. A rich man should not belie his resources by living the life of a pauper. Christians, too, must live up to their name and resources. Some "blaspheme that worthy Name by the which ye are called", James ii. 7, but we must not blaspheme it by any vestige of unworthy character or conduct. By the grace of GOD, are we "called saints"? Then, by that same grace, we are "called to be saints". Paul follows this up with a further description—

He calls them "faithful brethren", 2. The apostle was always careful about the words he used, and commonly invested even the most usual of them with deep significance. When he says "brethren", he means just that—it is not merely formal for him, as it so often is with us. These Christians are brothers and sisters because they "are all the children of GOD by faith in CHRIST JESUS", Galatians iii. 26. That basic fact, whatever be our country, clime, or colour, whatever be our denomination, constitutes all Christians as "*brethren*"—whatever our outward differences we are all alike bound together by the tie of our individual family relationship to our Heavenly Father. But that raises an enquiry in our minds. Are we "*faithful brethren*"? In some human families there is little evidence of a spirit of fidelity—rancour in the home, selfish purpose of individual interests, no love, no loyalty. Can it be so among the members of the Family of GOD? Well, what about ourselves? How delightful is that opposite picture of the harmony that should prevail, wherein "whether one member suffer, all the members suffer with it; or one member be honoured, all the members rejoice with it", 1 Corinthians xii. 26. As the late beloved, epigrammatic Bishop Taylor Smith used to say, "Each for all, and all for each." While we Christians are to be helpful, so far as we may, to those outside the family, we are to be particularly mindful of the welfare of each other, "as we have therefore opportunity, let us do good unto all men, and especially unto them who are of the household of faith", Galatians vi. 10. "Learn first to shew piety at home", says 1 Timothy v. 4. Our apostle was glad to have evidence among the Colossian believers of family fidelity: loyalty to one another, and loyalty to the one Father. Timothy, whose name he joins with his own in addressing this letter, was just a "brother", who in spite of his delicate health, 1 Timothy v. 23, remained, through thick and thin, so loyal to his big brother, Paul. One other thing the apostle says about these Colossian friends of his—

He describes them as "in CHRIST", 2. Oh yes, I know they were "at Colossæ"—breathing the fœtid atmosphere of this typically pagan city. How could the fair flowers of fidelity and holiness flourish in such a place? Only because they enjoyed the nearer, purer air of being "in CHRIST". The clever little water beetle is able to live in the muddy bed of the pond because it has the gift of weaving around itself a bubble of air. Thus it takes its own atmosphere down with it. I often invent a "let's pretend" story of a man shipwrecked on a desert island, who, happening to have his fountain pen still in his pocket, decides to write a message on a large island leaf to send to his people. Having thrown it into the sea, he could then only wait, and hope for the best. But, silly man, the leaf will soon be pulped and the message obliterated by the ocean. Oh, I forgot to mention that on his island he happened to find a bottle with a sealing top. So his S O S reached home, and led to his rescue, because though it was in the sea, it was in the bottle. Yes, although these Christians were in that Colossian sea of iniquity, they were kept safe and saintly because they were "in CHRIST". It is one of Paul's chief inspired conceptions, so often re-iterated through all his correspondence, that we are "in Him", "in the Lord", "in CHRIST". What amazing privilege and prediction is here! "CHRIST in you, the hope of glory", he says in Colossians i. 27; and now it is the other side of the blessed truth: you in CHRIST, the hope of safety. Before we finish our meditation on this brief opening of the letter, let us look at one more indication of this man's tenderness of approach to these people—

The Charming Nature of his Greetings

It was said by Dr. Johnson of Oliver Goldsmith that "he touched nothing that he did not adorn". It was in large measure true of our apostle. As we have seen, he used common words, and gave to them their true significance. He would not lightly have said, "Farewell": he would have meant from his heart, Fare well on the journey. "Good-bye" would never have been said formally, but in the fundamental sense of it, God-be-w'-ye. And now he dictates ordinary words of greeting, but how out-of-the-ordinary they sound on his lips.

"Grace" is the Gentile salutation—and to him who was the special apostle of the Gentiles, in token whereof he had adopted his Greek name of "Paul", and who was now writing to this Gentile church of Colossæ, it was only natural that he should hail them thus in their familiar way. But how much it means! God's *attitude,* as in Ephesians ii. 8; God's *assistance,* as in 1 Corinthians xv. 10; God's *attractiveness,* as in Acts iv. 33. Since all this is what the word implies, what a wish it is with which to greet our fellows: may this all-embracing grace be yours. "The true grace of God wherein ye stand", 1 Peter v. 12. Be it noted that in our passage this grace is connected with the first two Persons of the Holy Trinity—shall we say that God the Father is the source of it, and God the Son is the channel of it.

"Peace" is the Jewish greeting—and this man whose natural name was the Hebrew "Saul" was ever mindful of his brethren of the elect nation, who in his missionary journeyings always in every city went first to the Jews in their synagogue, and had a deep longing for their eternal welfare, "Brethren, my heart's desire and prayer to God for Israel is, that they might be saved", Romans x. 1. It is only to be expected that he would be happy to use the Israelite salutation—and to use it with all its deep

intention. Look at the word. It is not a surface word, but is concerned with things and conditions underneath. It is not merely a calm spirit when all goes well—that is something easily understandable; but Christian peace is an experience "which passeth all understanding", Philippians iv. 7. It can hold the ocean depths of a man's soul at rest when hurricanes disturb the surface of his life. This is veritably a "peace of GOD" which springs from a right relationship to the "GOD of peace", Philippians iv. 7, 9. GOD the Father is the embodiment of it; GOD the Son is the enduement of it. "This Man shall *be* the peace", Micah v. 5. In Old Testament days they had a formal greeting, often embodied in their correspondence—"Perfect peace, and at such a time," Ezra vii. 12: it connoted merely, at the present time, without any particular reference to the character of the times; but what significance attaches to it, if we use it in the light of what we have been saying —that we can, even at "such a time", enjoy perfect peace.

So ends Paul's tactful approach to his readers. What a tactful man he was. And how tactful the soul-winner needs to be, lest he put off the very people that he so zealously seeks to win to GOD. Let us only beware that we become so tactful that we do nothing, and say nothing.

> "Full salvation! Full salvation!
> Lo, the fountain opened wide,
> Streams through every land and nation
> From the Saviour's wounded side.
>   Full salvation!
> Streams an endless crimson tide."

HIS COURTEOUS ADDRESS

COLOSSIANS I. 3-11

Courteous Address

3 We give thanks to God and the Father of our Lord Jesus Christ, praying always for you,

4 Since we heard of your faith in Christ Jesus, and of the love *which ye have* to all the saints,

5 For the hope which is laid up for you in heaven, whereof ye heard before in the word of the truth of the gospel;

6 Which is come unto you, as *it is* in all the world; and bringeth forth fruit, as *it doth* also in you, since the day ye heard *of it,* and knew the grace of God in truth:

7 As ye also learned of Epaphras our dear fellow-servant, who is for you a faithful minister of Christ;

8 Who also declared unto us your love in the Spirit.

9 For this cause we also, since the day we heard *it,* do not cease to pray for you, and to desire that ye might be filled with the knowledge of his will in all wisdom and spiritual understanding;

10 That ye might walk worthy of the Lord unto all pleasing, being fruitful in every good work, and increasing in the knowledge of God;

11 Strengthened with all might, according to his glorious power, unto all patience and longsuffering with joyfulness;

HIS COURTEOUS ADDRESS
I. 3–11

OUR apostle now gets to the object and purpose of his writing; and he continues in that strain of the good manners of the perfect gentleman which we have already observed. He proceeds with agreeable Christian courtesy, and expresses first—

HIS DELIGHT, 3–5*

"We give thanks to GOD for you." It is to be noted that Paul strikes this note so often at the beginning of his letters, even in the case of 1 Corinthians, in which he is going to rebuke those Christians so severely for the low level of their lives. It is evidently his custom to look for something good in people, and he does not hesitate to give expression to it. Neither, on the other hand, does he allow these good points to blind him to the fundamental weakness and wickedness of the human heart—"there is none that doeth good, no, not one", Romans iii. 12. In spite of flashes of goodness, there is fundamental badness, which needs to be dealt with—can only be dealt with—by the grace, and gospel, of GOD, in whose saving efficacy Paul glories, Romans i. 16. Well, now, what are the things which he praises in this Colossian church?

Their "faith". The relationship between faith, or belief, and the Lord JESUS is expressed, in the Greek, by various prepositions. In Acts xvi. 31, "Believe *on* the Lord JESUS CHRIST", it is $\dot{\epsilon}\pi\iota$, whose significance may be pictorially suggested as resting on a foundation. In Acts xx. 21, "faith *toward* our Lord JESUS CHRIST", we have $\epsilon\dot{\iota}\varsigma$, which may not unjustly be thought of as conveying the idea of coming home, to find our dwelling-place in Him—"abide in Me",

John xv. 4. And now here in our passage, "faith *in* CHRIST JESUS", the word is "in", as if we had come to anchor in Him—"as an anchor of the soul, both sure and stedfast, and which entereth into that within the veil", Hebrews vi. How infinitely blessed is the intimate relationship with Him which He has so graciously allowed our faith to secure for us—our *Foundation*, on which all our security rests; our *Home*, in which all our joys and privileges are enjoyed; our *Anchor*, which keeps us safely riding the storms of life. And what next?

Their "love". Note that it is "the love that ye have to all the saints". It is, of course, a *Christian* quality, for it comes after faith, which makes them Christians in the first place. There is a kind of love whose Greek equivalent, ἐρος, is not found in the New Testament. It is a merely physical, sensual thing, a parody of the real thing. It is the subject of so many silly, nauseating songs of to-day. No, indeed, the Bible will have nothing to do with it. There is another kind, φίλος, wholly admirable in its degree—one might term it family love, or the love of friends; but it is only a human affection. This, however, that Paul speaks of is ἀγαπη, a divine quality. It is a *complete* quality, embracing "all the saints", and some even of the saints are not easily lovable. Moreover, it is a *commanded* quality, not something about which we can make our choice—"This is His commandment, that we should believe on the Name of His Son JESUS CHRIST, and love one another, as He gave us commandment", 1 John iii. 23. It is a *compassable* quality, therefore, since He never expects us to do what we can't; and the secret of this attitude toward folk is given us plainly —"the love of GOD is shed abroad in our hearts by the HOLY GHOST who is given unto us", Romans v. 5. We ought: therefore, we can: therefore, we will? Notice our verse 8, "Who hath declared unto us your love in the SPIRIT": there lie the Spring, and the Secret, and the Strength of this all-powerful virtue—"the fruit of the

SPIRIT", Galatians v. 22. And now Paul cites a further cause for his thankfulness—

Their "hope". Read, not "for", but "through", as in the original, as if this hope possessed a causal character, as if it were a part source of the love he has just been speaking of, and indeed, of the faith he mentioned in the earlier part of the paragraph. This hope is so frequently tied up with the fact of the Second Advent—"that blessed hope", as Titus ii. 13 calls it. Many have accused this subject as encouraging an impractical star-gazing attitude to life; and indeed, it could minister to that outlook. In fact, that did happen in the case of some of the Thessalonian believers; and this was probably why Paul wrote his First Epistle to them, to correct this very tendency. The New Testament leaves us in no doubt that, rightly and healthily held, the doctrine of the Return of our Lord possesses an ethical value second to none among all the teachings of Holy Scripture—"through" its influence many Christian virtues flourish. This will naturally lead on to a consideration of the second theme in Paul's mind here—

HIS DECLARATION, 5b–8

It concerns "the word of the truth of the gospel"—a matter always uppermost in his thoughts, and which was indeed the very mainspring of all his magnificent life and service. He was "separated unto the gospel of GOD", Romans i. 1—that meant everything to this intrepid missionary adventurer. What, then, has he to say about this gospel in our present passage? It is—

The original gospel—"whereof ye heard before", 5; that is, at the first. The old gospel, as contrasted with any new-fangled gospel, such as was being propagated in certain quarters in the Colossian church. If you wanted to rouse Paul's ire, you had only to start proclaiming a rival so-called gospel. Listen to him in Galatians i. 6–9—"if any man preach any other gospel unto you, let him be accursed". Blessed intolerance! The gospel of Do your best, the gospel of accumulated merit, the gospel of personal worth, the gospel of ritual observance—away with them, and all like them. They flatter to deceive, and can never avail to save a soul. By all the repeated emphasis of Divine revelation, it is only Paul's "gospel of the grace of GOD" that can accomplish the saving work. Like Jacob's ladder, it is brought within reach of man, "set up on the earth"—and "it reached" to heaven, Genesis xxviii. 12. And when our Lord JESUS came to earth to be our Ladder to the Skies, John i. 51, thank GOD "it reached". All other ladders, however attractive in themselves, fall short. The fact is that He is not a way to heaven, but "the" Way, as He Himself told us, John xiv. 6—the only way, the true way, the living way.

The universal gospel—"which is come unto you, as it is in all the world", 6. It was this same writer who declared, "I am not ashamed of the gospel of CHRIST, for it is the power of GOD unto salvation to everyone that believeth, to the Jew first, and also to the Greek", Romans i. 16. Down through the years it has proved itself indigenous in all lands, it has settled itself down as native to all races, it is at home in every clime and age, it has flourished in its conquests of human hearts throughout the wide world. By the way, it was when some Greeks desired to see Him that the Saviour used words that express the very heart of the gospel, "I, if I be lifted up from the earth will draw all men unto Me", John xii. 32—that is, *not "all" without exception*, for that has manifestly not been so, *but "all" without distinction*: Greeks as well as Jews. The appeal and efficacy of His atoning death is without frontiers, and will prove to have embraced "a great multitude, which no man could number, of all nations, and kindreds, and peoples, and tongues [which] stood before the throne, and before the Lamb", Revelation vii. 9. Oh, then, to fall in line with this mighty purpose of GOD, and to be truly missionary-hearted Christians, like this Paul himself.

The vital gospel—"bringeth forth fruit", 6. All that we have seen thus far has emphasized for us that the gospel is a living force. Stories could be multiplied of instances wherein the sound, or sight, of a gospel word, without any human explanation, has brought about the complete conversion of an erstwhile godless and careless soul. One recalls the case of a man doing some repair work high up in the old Crystal Palace building. All of a sudden, he heard distinctly words, coming seemingly from nowhere, which changed his whole life with GOD'S salvation—the words, "Behold the Lamb of GOD, which taketh away the sin of the world", John i. 29. The story is that C. H. Spurgeon was engaged to preach at a great rally to be held at the Crystal Palace, and the previous day he went to the place to try out his voice in the great auditorium, and to test himself he just declaimed that gospel verse, with the result we have mentioned. Many such incidents could be recounted, to demonstrate the vital "power . . . unto salvation" of this Divine good news.

The personal gospel—"which is come unto you", 6. Be it proclaimed to the multitude, it yet is presented to the individual. The prophetic statement of Old Testament deliverance is also a principle of New Testament salvation, "Ye shall be gathered one by one", Isaiah xxvii. 12. "What must *I* do to be saved?" Acts xvi. 30. "What shall *I* do then with JESUS?" Matthew xxvii. 22. Well then, let this suffice for our consideration of Paul's great declaration of the gospel, and let us go on to—

HIS DESIRE, 9–11

In his Christian courtesy, he reveals to these friends a big secret. As we have suggested, he has never seen them; and, in any case, there in Rome he is many miles, of land and sea, away from them—but he now opens his heart to them, and tells them that they are often in his mind, and better still, in his prayers, "we do not cease to pray for you", 9. He has heard from their friend and leader Epaphras (7) of their faith, and love and hope, and so he lets them know that, because he is well aware of the enervating influences of a heathen atmosphere, as in Colossæ, he is giving himself continually to prayer for them, that those estimable qualities may be deepened, and strengthened. And, tell me: what better could anyone do for another than to pray for them? To the end, therefore, of their well-being, he opens his heart to them, and reveals to them the pattern of his prayers, his "desire" for them. Note the recurrence of that word "all"—which almost appears to indicate what is the complete Christian.

"*All wisdom*", 9. (a) The "knowledge" here referred to is not of a merely formal or superficial kind, but of a deeper, more thorough sort, since a prepositional addition is made to the simple word here in the original, which indicates this. (b) It is, further, spiritual knowledge that Paul's prayer seeks for them, "spiritual understanding", as he calls it. "The eyes of your understanding being enlightened", he puts it, in Ephesians i. 18. (c) It is, indeed, a growing knowledge—"increasing in the knowledge", he says. Are we growing thus? In "the knowledge of His will"—for ourselves, for the Kingdom, and for things at large. All this is to be had by a continual study of His will as revealed in His Word, until, in ever-widening measure, "we have the mind of CHRIST", 1 Corinthians ii. 16. A deeper aspect of Christian knowledge now emerges —"the knowledge of GOD": not merely of His things, even of His will, but of Himself. The acquaintance with people generally proceeds in orderly sequence. (a) First, there is *Introduction*—and this came to us when first we came to CHRIST. How interesting is the story of Peter's introduction to Him, John i. 40–2. Have we, then, been introduced? (b) Then, there is to be *Increase*—the theme of our present meditation. We see it developing in Peter from the time when the Master came to him subsequently, and called

him to "Follow Me", Matthew iv. 19. (c) All which can
lead up to *Intimacy*—so beautifully demonstrated in Peter's
case, along with his two fellow-apostles, James and John,
in Jairus' house, on the Transfiguration Mount, and in the
Gethsemane garden. Let us make no mistake, the Lord has
no favourites, but He has intimates, who are prepared to
pay the cost in absolute devotion, and complete consecra-
tion. You will recall that, in Philippians iii. 10, the apostle
tells us that in his pursuance of knowledge, his chief ambition was, "that I may know Him". Such close fellowship
and understanding embodies "all wisdom", indeed!

"All pleasing," 10. We affirm that it is no necessary
mark of high spirituality that we are unpleasing to the
worldlings. Rather, let us, within Christian limits, hope to
be popular with our fellows, and seek to use such "pleasing" to make an impact upon them for GOD. Yet we must
keep our eyes open to the lurking danger of such a popularity—lest in winning the world's smile we come to lose
the Lord's smile, which means everything to the earnest
Christian. When Paul is writing under the figure of the
Christian as a soldier, he brings out this point when he
says, "No man that warreth [that is, is engaged in active
service] entangleth himself with the affairs of this life [that
is, ordinary and civil life, seeing there's a war on], that he
may please Him who hath chosen him to be a soldier",
2 Timothy ii. 4. If he can please others, well and good;
but his chief and over-riding loyalty must be to his
Sovereign, "that he may please *Him*". Such "all pleasing"
is to be secured by our "walk", that is to be worthy of Him,
in all we do, and are; and by our "work", which is to be
worth-while, good, and serviceable to the Kingdom. Self-
pleasing is, of course, right out of court for a Christian.

"All might," 11, comes next in our contemplation of this
complete Christian. Whenever we come across a description of what a believer's character and conduct are to be
like, we are inclined to be halted by such high demands.

A worthy walk, and a worth-while work—yes, indeed; but how? Let us ever bear this in mind as a principle of the spiritual life, that "If GOD command thee so, then thou shalt be able to", Exodus xviii. 23. In other words, if I know that I ought, I know that I can. "All might" is available to me, so that "I can do all things [He requires] through CHRIST which strengtheneth me", Philippians iv. 13. So does our passage answer our trembling "How?" Note that it is a continuous power—"strengtheneth" is a present participle, being strengthened—it goes on, ever at our disposal. Moreover, it is a sufficient power—"according to His glorious power": we might render the phrase, "up to the limit of His power". I fancy that, however great our need, it will never exceed that limit. In another place, our apostle changes the metaphor to say, "My GOD shall supply all your need according to His riches in glory by CHRIST JESUS", Philippians iv. 19—His blank cheque to be drawn on the inexhaustible account in the Bank of Heaven. Surely we need never live spiritually bankrupt lives when such limitless resources are ours for the taking. We should be living as princes, not as paupers. What relief, then, and what rejoicing, comes with the realisation that for all Divine calls upon us we have "all might" to draw on.

"*All patience,*" 11. That means Christian stickability: the power to keep on keeping on. We shall have temptations to give up—the allurements of the world; the weakness of our resolve; the frequency of our failures; these, and other things, may tend to undermine our resistance. So Paul prays that these Colossian believers may have the grace of perseverance. It was an outstanding quality in an Old Testament saint, "Daniel purposed . . . and Daniel continued", Daniel i. 8, 21. It was an outstanding quality in the first New Testament saints, who "continued stedfastly", Acts ii. 42. Be it ours also to display a like tenacity—and that, not in a temper of grim and glum resignation, but "with joyfulness". What a grand note to finish on!

HIS MAIN EMPHASIS

Main Emphasis

12 Giving thanks unto the Father, which hath made us meet to be partakers of the inheritance of the saints in light:

13 Who hath delivered us from the power of darkness, and hath translated *us* into the kingdom of his dear Son:

14 In whom we have redemption through his blood, *even* the forgiveness of sins:

15 Who is the image of the invisible God, the firstborn of every creature:

16 For by him were all things created, that are in heaven, and that are in earth, visible and invisible, whether *they be* thrones, or dominions, or principalities, or powers: all things were created by him, and for him:

17 And he is before all things, and by him all things consist.

18 And he is the head of the body, the church: who is the beginning, the firstborn from the dead; that in all *things* he might have the preeminence.

19 For it pleased *the Father* that in him should all fulness dwell;

20 And, having made peace through the blood of his cross, by him to reconcile all things unto himself; by him, *I say,* whether *they be* things in earth, or things in heaven.

21 And you, that were sometime alienated and enemies in *your* mind by wicked works, yet now hath he reconciled

22 In the body of his flesh through death, to present you holy and unblameable and unreproveable in his sight:

23 If ye continue in the faith grounded and settled, and *be* not moved away from the hope of the gospel, which ye have heard, *and* which was preached to every creature which is under heaven; whereof I Paul am made a minister;

24 Who now rejoice in my sufferings for you, and fill up that which is behind of the afflictions of Christ in my flesh for his body's sake, which is the church:

25 Whereof I am made a minister, according to the dispensation of God which is given to me for you, to fulfil the word of God;

26 *Even* the mystery which hath been hid from ages and from generations, but now is made manifest to his saints:

27 To whom God would make known what *is* the riches of the glory of this mystery among the Gentiles; which is Christ in you, the hope of glory:

28 Whom we preach, warning every man, and teaching every man in all wisdom; that we may present every man perfect in Christ Jesus:

29 Whereunto I also labour, striving according to his working, which worketh in me mightily.

HIS MAIN EMPHASIS
I. 12–29

THE passage is so full that we cannot deal with all the points and matters raised; but we shall not go far wrong if we say that the great theme throughout is CHRIST. That, after all, is the subject of the whole Bible. Certain native Christians used to call it the "JESUS Book"—a beautifully instinctive assessment of its contents. (1) In the Old Testament, we have *Preparation*, for His coming. (2) In the Gospels, we have *Presentation*, He has come, here He is. (3) In the Acts, we have *Proclamation*, the message of the gospel of His grace and salvation. (4) In the Epistles, we have *Personification*, "for me to live is CHRIST". (5) In the Revelation, we have *Predomination*, the Lamb on the throne. Yes, the whole book is, fundamentally, about Him. Open the volume where you will, and you will find Him. An Ethiopian is puzzling over an abstruse passage in Isaiah liii about a lamb being led to the slaughter. He can't understand what it means; but Philip, "beginning at that same Scripture, preached unto him JESUS", Acts viii. 35. Our Lord overtakes two grief-stricken disciples who are mystified at the death of their beloved Master and Friend, and resolves their problem, "beginning at Moses, and all the prophets, He expounded unto them in all the Scriptures the things concerning Himself", Luke xxiv. 27. In the light of all this, we are not surprised to learn that, in this passage now before us, the theme, and stress, is about Him.

THE UNIQUENESS OF HIS BEING

Look down at those verses 15–18, and note some of the descriptive names given to CHRIST.

"The Image," 15. "No man hath seen GOD at any time," 1 John iv. 12 reminds us. Do you recall how, when Moses asked to see GOD'S glory, the Almighty replied, "Thou canst not see My face: for there shall no man see Me and live", Exodus xxxiii. 20? By the way, when, in Genesis xxxii. 30, Jacob said, "I have seen GOD face to face, and my life is preserved", I suggest that it was GOD the Son that he referred to, who, in coming to wrestle with the patriarch, assumed one of His pre-incarnation appearances, of which there are so many in the Old Testament; for He was the very Image of GOD. Do we wish to know what GOD is like? We may so do, for "he that hath seen Me hath seen the Father", John xiv. 9, said our Lord JESUS. And how moving it is to realise that we, too, may, in our measure, come to some degree of resemblance to Him—"we all, with open face, beholding as in a glass, the glory of GOD, are changed into the same Image, from glory to glory, even as by the SPIRIT of the Lord", 2 Corinthians iii. 18. One day we shall be perfectly like Him, "we shall be like Him, for we shall see Him as He is", 1 John iii. 2; but meanwhile we seek, through obedience to the Word, and to the SPIRIT, a growing likeness down here. But, oh miracle of the Advent, that such as we shall be such as He! King Charles wrote a book—or, as some say, his chaplain wrote it—which was called "Eikon Basilike", the Image of a King, setting forth the prime qualities of kingly character and behaviour. Unfortunately he did not fulfil, in his own person, the high ideals of his book. For ourselves, as Christians, Romans v. 17 says "They shall reign in life": we have the name, is our personality the same? Is there anything kingly about our character?

"The First-born," 15. The name accords Him the *priority.* We look round upon "every creature", every created thing, and we know He was there first. The description seems to cling to Him. At His incarnation, it is recorded that "she brought forth her first-born Son", Luke ii. 7. There were

other children of Mary, as we learn from Matthew xiii. 55–6, but He was first. Of His resurrection, our passage speaks of Him as "the first-born from the dead", 18. Others were, before Him, miraculously brought back from the dead, but they all died again eventually—they were not true resurrections but resuscitations. His was the first real rising for ever, "CHRIST being raised from the dead dieth no more", Romans vi. 9. Yes, His is the priority: should He not also be Priority No. 1 in every Christian's life? But our phrase also carries the idea of *superiority*. In speaking of Him, John the Baptist says, not only that "He was before me", in priority, but that He "is preferred before me", in superiority, John i. 30. Superior in moral splendour, superior in saving power, superior in practical guidance, superior in transforming influence, superior in gracious friendship, John xv. 14. Shall we not also "prefer" Him to all other people and things, "the chiefest among ten thousand", Song of Solomon v. 10? But we have not yet done with His uniqueness.

"The Creator", 16. "By Him were all things created." Yes; but look back to Genesis i. 1, "In the beginning GOD created": the word for the Deity is "Elohim", a plural word, which is said by the commentators to be understood as the plural of majesty—as a king speaks of himself in his proclamations as "we"; but is it not more than that? Can we not see in it the plural of trinity: GOD, at the very start of His revelation to man, introducing Himself as the Trinity in the Unity—a matter never discussed, nor explained, anywhere in the Bible, but always assumed and taken for granted. Our finite minds could not, as yet, understand this infinite truth, therefore GOD has not disclosed it; but, as Robert Browning says—

"GOD, stooping,
Shews sufficient of His light
For us to rise by—and I rise."

Well now, it is clear that all Three Persons are concerned with the great enterprise of Creation. (1) GOD created— GOD the Father was in it. (2) "The SPIRIT of GOD moved upon the face of the waters", Genesis i. 2—GOD the SPIRIT was in it. (3) "All things were made by Him", John i. 3— GOD the Son was in it; GOD "the Word" (cf. "GOD *said*", Genesis i. 3). Our Lord, it would seem, was, in that early dispensation, the Executive of the Godhead. Is that why He so frequently comes to the aid of men in His pre-incarnation appearances, as to Abraham, Moses, Joshua, Gideon, Balaam and others? We would say that in this present Age, the HOLY SPIRIT is the Executive of the Godhead. To return to our passage, there is particular point in Paul's reference to our Lord as the Creator. A certain false teaching, called Gnosticism, is being propagated in Colossian church circles. It would appear that it was to counteract this that Epaphras had gone to Rome to consult Paul, as we suggested in our first chapter. The basis of this heresy was that they held the inherent evil of matter, and that, therefore, the entirely holy GOD could not directly have created nor touched it. The only way for Him to act in the affair was to work through a descending and deteriorating series of agencies, angels, if you like, which these teachers called "æons". It is easy to see what havoc all this would wreak upon the Bible revelation if the bundle of errors were accepted. So Paul, master-tactician that he was, loses no time in stating explicitly, and categorically, that "all things were created by Him", definitely and directly. And it would seem that His creative activity will be evidenced also in the Age of the New Jerusalem, for "Behold, I make all things new," Revelation xxi. 5. And it is certainly at work in this Age in the hearts and lives of men, for "if any man be in CHRIST, he is a new creation", 2 Corinthians v. 17 (see Moffatt). A Creator, indeed!

"*The Head*," 18. "He is the Head of the body." Under what impulses, instructions, and influences does your body function? The answer is, of course, clear to us all: the direction of all our movement, whether of the body as a whole, or of any particular part, comes from the brain, the head. Under the figure of the body corporate, the church—"the blessed company of all faithful people", as the Prayer Book defines it—is taught to look upon CHRIST as the Instigator and Controller of all its actions, whether as the company, or as individuals. Each believer has a privileged place in the body, and a specific function therein —"ye are the body of CHRIST, and members in particular", 1 Corinthians xii. 27. Some are there for manual work— "the hand"; some for pedal work—"the foot"; some for optical work—"the eye"; some for aural work—"the ear"; some even for nasal work—else "where were the smelling?" verse 17; there are people whose olfactory nerve is highly sensitive, who have a rare sense of smell for detecting false doctrine—very useful members of the body! Not least so in this Colossian church, now threatened with infection. Our main point here is that every member is to be motivated and moved by the Head. May none of us become paralysed limbs, but be quick to respond to the dictates of the Head—"that in all things He might have the pre-eminence". Now, in following Paul's emphasis, we consider—

THE UPSHOT OF HIS WORK

"*Redemption*," 12–14. (*a*) The price of it, "through His blood". Some people seem to think that we have to pay for our redemption, while all the time it has already been paid for. No amount of good deeds, no reckoning of good character, could avail to purchase our redemption—"not by works of righteousness which we have done, but according to His mercy He saved us", Titus iii. 5. We do not earn it as "wages", we receive it as "the gift of GOD", Romans vi. 23. (*b*) The pardon of it—"even the forgiveness of sins": blessed release from an evil conscience, and an eternal doom. This is, of course, the first upshot of His work of redemption. The primary nature of this blessing is, as we know, strikingly illustrated in the familiar story of the man sick of the palsy (poor fellow, we are not surprised that he was sick of it). Before ever the Master dealt with his body, He went down to the fundamental need of his soul. "Son, be of good cheer, thy sins be forgiven thee," Matthew ix. 2. Was it that his illness was caused by sin; or was it that, lying so long on his bed, he had had time to think, and had become convicted of his sinfulness? It would seem that he was worrying about that; and that he would have been "of good cheer", even if he had gone back without bodily healing. Yes, His forgiveness is our prime necessity. Another thing. (c) The positive side of it— "the inheritance", 12; "the kingdom", 13. Believers are privileged indeed, seeing that they are, negatively, brought out, and, positively, brought in. "He brought us out, that He might bring us in," Deuteronomy vi. 23. We have *a share in a glorious inheritance* along with all the believers in Him who is "the Light", John viii. 12, together with all such who have passed on into the Eternal Light beyond —an inheritance comprising all the joys, all the blessings, all the riches that are in CHRIST for Here, and for Hereafter. "If children, then heirs; heirs of GOD, and joint-heirs with CHRIST," Romans viii. 17. But are we indeed "meet" to be partakers of such bounty? No; not in the sense of being worthy of it, but the word properly means "qualified"—not on our own account, but by His infinite mercy, and sovereign grace, we are qualified to be beneficiaries of His so blessed Will and Testament. And further, we have *a place in a wondrous kingdom.* "Translated" from the rebellious and dark sway of the usurper into the all-blessed realm of Him "whose right it is" to reign, Ezekiel xxi. 27, a kingdom of "righteousness, and peace, and joy", Romans xiv. 17. Blessed are the subjects of such a Sovereign. "Happy are thy men, happy are these thy servants," 1 Kings x. 8, said Sheba's queen to King Solomon.

Thrice happy they who serve "a greater than Solomon",
Matthew xii. 42. But stay a moment: we say a lot, and
sing a lot about His kingship, but, as a matter of fact, is
it a reality in our own lives? Many years ago there was a
great conference in Liverpool of the Student Volunteer
Missionary Union. At the last moment an expected dele-
gation of students from Japan found it impossible to come,
so they sent a message, which thrilled the great gathering;
it consisted of three words, "Make JESUS King". That
summer a brilliant young Cambridge undergraduate, Russell
Darbyshire, who afterwards became Archbishop of Cape-
town, was leading the seaside services of the Children's
Special Service Mission at Swanage, and wrote for them a
special chorus—

> "Make JESUS King, through Him we shall live,
>> Our souls and our bodies to Him we will give.
> His praises we'll sing, and others we'll bring
>> Till the whole of creation shall make JESUS King."

One added thing is mentioned here, as part of the outcome
of His work.

"*Reconciliation*," 20–3. (*a*) "*All things*," 20. To grasp
the real significance of this verse, I think we must go back
to the dramatic happening of Genesis iii, where we find
that, in consequence of man's Fall, the whole universe was
put out of joint. The vegetable realm was, for the first
time, invaded by weeds, "thorns and thistles", 18—awaiting
the day of reconciliation, when "instead of the thorn shall
come up the fir tree, and instead of the brier shall come
up the myrtle tree", Isaiah lv. 13. The animal world shall
exchange its domestic tameness, as observed when "GOD
. . . brought [every beast of the field] unto Adam, to see
what he would call them", for the fierceness which so
many now possess, until the day of reconciliation, when
"they shall not hurt nor destroy in all My holy mountain",
Isaiah lxv. 25. "For the earnest expectation of the creatures

waiteth for the manifestation of the sons of GOD . . ."
Romans viii. 19-22. And all this reconcilement is, be it
noted, "through the Blood of His cross". The malady is
the consequence of sin; and the Blood, the salvation from
sin, will be the remedy whereby the maladjusted joints of
the natural world shall be set right again. (b) "And you," 21.
Enemies that we were, He "died for us", Romans v. 10,
and through that death, "reconciled us to GOD", which
holy estate is ours if "we have now received the reconciliation", verse 11, R.V. In which latter case, He has entrusted
us with the privilege and responsibility of bearing to others
the "word", the message of reconciliation, as "ambassadors", speaking in His Name, 2 Corinthians v. 18-21.
Let us, then, "continue" (back to Colossians i. 23) to hold
and proclaim that faith, so that He shall never have to
reprove us for fostering, and furthering, another "gospel".
Well now, can we ever be too thankful for all that His
redemption, and His reconciliation, through His precious
Blood, means for us? Shall not our gratitude be shewn in—

THE UNDERTAKING OF HIS SERVICE

The Lord CHRIST is still the prevailing theme of our
passage; and here the apostle unfolds for us the duty and
delight of serving Him. Not that that service was ever
easy for him. Over and over again he calls himself, and is
proud to call himself, "a bond-slave of JESUS CHRIST",
e.g., Romans i. 1, Gk., and that figure implies an "all-in"
energy, and an "all-out" endeavour for the Master "whose
service is", for all that, "perfect freedom", as the Prayer
Book has it. Listen, then, to this outstanding labourer,
1 Corinthians xv. 10, while he commends to us—

A readiness to suffer, 24. There is something very
difficult in this verse. What does Paul mean by "fill up that
which is behind of the afflictions of CHRIST"? It just cannot mean that the apostle thinks of himself as supple-
menting anything lacking in the Saviour's atoning suffering.

That would be wholly contrary to his teaching about the completeness and sufficiency of the Calvary offering, as it would also be contrary to the Master's own triumphant cry, "It is finished", John xix. 30. No! Greatly daring, in the face of the scholars, I am going to venture to say what I think. May we not paraphrase the verse, "Fulfil what yet remains of the appointed tale of afflictions that I must suffer for CHRIST'S sake, and for the advancement of His church". One cannot help recalling that prognostication of the Master's concerning him at the time of his conversion, "I will shew him how great things he must suffer for My Name's sake", Acts ix. 16. Was he, then, made aware of what was to befall him in the service of the One whose Name he had so violently persecuted, and which now he was so earnestly to proclaim? And was he now aware, as he wrote from his imprisonment, that the limit had not yet been reached? Of all this it is difficult to be sure; but one thing is quite certain, that this intrepid missionary was ready, even joyfully ready, to "endure hardness as a good soldier of JESUS CHRIST", 2 Timothy ii. 3. And yet some of us—weaklings that we are—curl up at the very thought of what others may think, or say, or do! Is there one of us who is not amazed at the catalogue of sufferings that Paul records in 2 Corinthians xi. 23–28; and are there not some of us who have almost a feeling of shame that our allegiance to CHRIST has cost us so little? Are we, then, ready, if needs be, to suffer for His Name?

A readiness to spread the news, 28. When, in verse 23, he speaks of the gospel being preached to "every creature", he is not thinking along the lines of St. Francis of Assisi preaching to the birds. He means, every kind of creature— that is, every kind of person. We find persons as creatures, for example, in 2 Corinthians v. 17. He has the widest conception of the gospel's reach—"every man . . . every man . . . every man". To that end, he surely must have been one of the most prolific travellers of his time—and no cars, no trains, no planes. "So, as much as in me is, I am ready to preach the gospel to you that are at Rome," Romans i. 15. He was always anxious to get to that Imperial City, the very hub of the then world. He was a great strategist, and spent so much of his tireless energy in big, metropolitan towns, from which the influence could reach out to many directions near and far. But oh! for Rome. Well, GOD promised him that, "Be of good cheer, Paul, for as thou hast testified of Me in Jerusalem, so must thou bear witness also at Rome", Acts xxiii. 11. Yet, how differently was the witness eventually given from what the apostle imagined. In Rome, yes; but in prison—but how faithfully and fruitfully the witness was borne, through his correspondence (as this very letter to Colossians), and through his many contacts. Are we as eager to spread the Good Tidings? That great missionary, the late Mildred Cable, used to tell us that the greatest crime of the desert was to know where water was and not to tell it. One's mind travels back to far Samaria where four erstwhile desperately hungry men were revelling in an unexpected feast, and suddenly paused, and thought of starving people in the city, "We do not well; this is a day of good tidings [a Gospel Day], and we hold our peace", 2 Kings vii. 9. Do we? Or are we keen to get to dying souls news of the Bread of Life, the Water of Life?

A readiness to strive hard, 29. "Labour" is the word he uses. Among the ranks of the Christians there are workers and shirkers. There is no doubt of the category to which Paul belonged. He was so imbued with the HOLY SPIRIT that "he could no other". Notice his explanation, "striving according to His working, which worketh in me mightily". After all, it is always the inner that governs the outer—and it little avails us to try to whip our energy to work harder for GOD. That may succeed for a moment, but it will soon exhaust itself, and we shall revert to "tepid" again. Paul's enthusiasm abides, and abounds. Why?

Listen to him, "I laboured more abundantly than they all; yet not I, but the grace of GOD that was with me", 1 Corinthians xv. 10. Listen again: "the love of CHRIST constraineth us", 2 Corinthians v. 14. And here in our passage, "His working . . . in me". All this is the motive-power—inward, and GODWARD: and therefore is available for us all. Let us, then, be up and doing. "Son, go work today in My vineyard," Matthew xxi. 28. "Be strong . . . and work, for I am with you," Haggai ii. 4. Thus, for all the service expected of us we can rely upon—

THE UTTERMOST OF HIS GRACE

Here is what Paul calls a "mystery", a word which, in the New Testament, does not bear the connotation that we usually attach to it. Rather does it indicate a something shrouded but awaiting disclosure: the unveiling has now come. "The mystery which has been hid from ages . . . but now is made manifest to the saints," 26. When our apostle speaks as he does of "the riches of this mystery", 27, I think he refers first to the wealth of the mercy and grace of the GOD who conceived and revealed such a wonderful proposition; and then to the wealth of spiritual experience wrapped up in the matter—the uttermost grace of the Giver; the uttermost grace for the Recipient. "GOD is able to make all grace abound toward you; that ye, always having all sufficiency in all things, may abound to every good thing," 2 Corinthians ix. 8. So what more do you want?

Yes; but what *is* this mystery that means so much to us? In three monosyllables—*multum in parvo*—it is, "CHRIST in you", 27. See that poker grown hot in the flames—the poker in the fire; yes, but the fire in the poker. Look at that bath—the sponge in the water; yes, but the water in the sponge. Think of yourself—the body in the air; yes, but the air in the body. Turn to John xv. 4—"abide in Me, and I in you". And now in this very Epistle the writer, using one of His favourite phrases, speaks of believers as being "in CHRIST", i. 2; while here in our passage it is "CHRIST in you"—in Him, for your salvation; in you, for your full salvation, with all the "riches" implied in such amazing grace. We do not wonder that in this portion, as through every part of the Letter, Paul's chief emphasis is CHRIST—and that the sum and stress of it all is that of Galatians ii. 20, "CHRIST liveth in me".

> "Oh, the glorious revelation!
> See the cleansing current flow,
> Washing stains of condemnation
> Whiter than the driven snow:
>   Full salvation!
> Oh, the rapturous bliss to know."

HIS ADVICE ON ADVANCE

Advice on Advance

1 For I would that ye knew what great conflict I have for you and for them at Laodicea, and *for* as many as have not seen my face in the flesh;

2 That their hearts might be comforted, being knit together in love, and unto all riches of the full assurance of understanding, to the acknowledgement of the mystery of God, and of the Father, and of Christ;

3 In whom are hid all the treasures of wisdom and knowledge.

4 And this I say, lest any man should beguile you with enticing words.

5 For though I be absent in the flesh, yet am I with you in the spirit, joying and beholding your order, and the stedfastness of your faith in Christ.

6 As ye have therefore received Christ Jesus the Lord, *so* walk ye in him:

7 Rooted and built up in him, and stablished in the faith, as ye have been taught, abounding therein with thanksgiving.

8 Beware lest any man spoil you through philosophy and vain deceit, after the tradition of men, after the rudiments of the world, and not after Christ.

9 For in him dwelleth all the fulness of the Godhead bodily.

10 And ye are complete in him, which is the head of all principality and power:

HIS ADVICE ON ADVANCE
II. 1–10

THERE are three "gets" for the Christian life—*Get out,*
from sin; *Get in,* to life in CHRIST; *Get on,* in full salvation in Him. Our present passage deals with this third.
For the underlying truth here is progress—pilgrim's progress, if you like. For Christianity is a "going" concern.
Think of the Master's three "go's". "Go home to thy
friends, and tell them," Mark v. 19. "Go out quickly into
the streets and lanes of the city . . . into the highways
and hedges, and compel [persuade] people to come in,"
Luke xiv. 21, 23. "Go ye into all the world, and preach
the gospel to every creature," Mark xvi. 15. There is, of
course, a legitimate time for pause—to seek rest, or repair,
or recuperation, or re-commissioning. You get a typological
illustration of that in the case of the children of Israel at
the Red Sea, where, through Moses, GOD gave them two
commands. First, "Stand still"; second, "Go forward",
Exodus xiv. 13, 15. The first only a preparation for the
second. So, though at times the Christian will wisely
stand still, he is never to come to a standstill. Says
Hebrews vi. 1, "Let us go on". Yes, let us!

WHEN WE SHALL BEGIN

"As ye have therefore received CHRIST JESUS the Lord,
so walk ye in Him," 6. (*a*) "Ye have". The Epistle is
addressed to Christians. You might as well tell a chair to
walk whose legs are lifeless as tell a non-Christian to do
so whose soul, as yet, is dead. But if "ye have", then ye can,
and should. (*b*) "Received"—that seems to be the New
Testament's normal way of indicating our side of the saving
transaction, as tantamount to that other word, so often

51

used, believe. "To as many as *received* Him, to them gave
He power to become the sons of GOD, even to them that
believe on His Name," John i. 12. Have you received Him
as your own Saviour? Perhaps you say you are not sure,
you can't put your finger on any specific moment? Well, do
you believe on Him, trust Him, as your Saviour? You do?
Same thing! "Ye have" (*c*) "the Lord". Let us never forget that He comes not only to be the Saviour of our soul,
but also the Lord of our life—in complete control of those
whom He has "bought with a price", 1 Corinthians vi. 20,
His blood-purchased possession, for His use, and His glory.

WHAT WE SHALL BECOME

Good learners, 2–3. Here is envisaged a group of students
"knit together" in a common purpose to pursue their studies
in their richly rewarding subject. The classroom is per-
vaded by a beautiful atmosphere, a spirit of love—love for
their fellow scholars, love for their studies, love for their
Master. The apostle writes that they may be "comforted",
that is, encouraged, in their pursuit. The aim, then, is that
they may have "all riches of the full assurance of understanding"—a difficult phrase, which Moffatt renders, "all
the wealth of conviction that comes from insight". These
people have got to combat the insidious false teaching that
is being spread around, and something more is needed
than the mere intellectual assent to the true doctrine—
there must be a real and deep conviction of the truth if
they are to do battle against error. Is it not always so,
even for us in our day and generation, for we, too, are
bidden to "fight the good fight of ["the", Gk.] faith",
1 Timothy vi. 12, and to "hold fast the form of sound
words", 2 Timothy i. 13. We take up the formula of our
Creed, the epitome of "the faith", and, clause by clause,
we declare our belief therein. Do we accept these statements merely because they have been handed down to us,
and it has become little more than a routine habit to

acknowledge them? In that event, we shall not have much inclination to "hold fast" to them, in the face of some questioning, nor to "fight" for them against the onslaughts of disbelief. Perhaps we have gone further. We have sought to examine these things in the light of modern scholarship, and are satisfied in our own minds that they are true. Good, so far as it goes; but it could be but a cold agreement of the mind. We shall not speak lightly of this attitude: the mind assuredly has its part to play— but something further is here called for. Through the frame of orthodoxy there needs to flow the red, pulsating blood of conviction, such a growing "understanding" of what lies behind, and within, these truths as shall capture the ardent enthusiasm of our whole being. Such a man will prove himself a faithful custodian, "I have kept the faith", and a doughty warrior, "I have fought the good fight", 2 Timothy iv. 7. Our apostle continues, "the acknowledgement of the mystery", or, as again Moffatt has it, "the open secret". What is this, once so hidden, and now so open? It would seem to refer to some relationship for this Age between GOD the Father, and GOD the Son, as if, in the counsels of the Triune GOD, it were determined that CHRIST should be for us the all-embracing Repository, as Divine Representative of the Deity, of all that we Christians can need, "In whom are hid all the treasures of wisdom and knowledge", 3. What a wondrous casket for all seekers after the knowledge of all the What, and the How, of the Christian life. Here, then, is advance, progress in knowledge—"then shall we know, if we follow on to know the Lord", Hosea vi. 3.

Good walkers, 6. How splendidly some people walk; how slovenly, others. This Epistle exhorts all true believers to "walk in Him". It is interesting to observe how frequently the walk is used to describe the Christian life. As we have noted earlier, the Christian life is not a sedentary occupation, but a pedestrian affair, a walk—often, a running; on rare occasions, even a flying, Isaiah xl. 31. If now we "walk in Him", we shall certainly "walk in love, as CHRIST also hath loved us", Ephesians v. 2. We shall "walk as children of light", Ephesians v. 8, following Him who is "the Light". We shall "walk worthy of the vocation wherewith ye are called", Ephesians iv. 1—like as a soldier would walk according to military tradition. We shall "walk in truth", 3 John 4, avoiding all pitfalls of error. We shall "walk in wisdom toward them that are without", Colossians iv. 5, lest that by anything we say, anything we do, anything we are, we should prove a stumbling block to any outside the fold. And, as the secret of it all, we shall "walk in the SPIRIT", Galatians v. 16, 25. He will be, if we let Him, the motive power, the driving force, seeing that "ye shall receive power after that the HOLY GHOST is come upon you", Acts i. 8. Before we leave this point, let us note that our walk is to be "in Him". What a difference atmosphere makes to our walking. How sprightly we become on a clear, bright morning, how lackadaisical we often are when the day is heavy and murky. Our Lord is here presented to us as our enveloping atmosphere, and our intimate environment, "for in Him we live, and move, and have our being", Acts xvii. 28—so especially and exactly true of all believers.

Good trees, 7. More than once godly folk are spoken of under the imagery of a tree. "He shall be like a tree", says Psalm i. 3, and goes on to catalogue some of the attractive features of it. *Its fountain,* "planted by the rivers of water", so that its roots draw into itself needful nourishment, and maintain in it that continual freshness which may be the happy experience of us all. *Its fruit,* "that bringeth forth his fruit in his season", the seasonable and delectable "fruit of the SPIRIT", Galatians v. 22, which the Heavenly Husbandman ever labours, and delights to see—fruit; more fruit; much fruit; lasting fruit, John xv. 2-5, 8, 16. *Its foliage,* "his leaf also shall not wither", giving abiding beauty of character to the tree, since "He will beautify the meek with salvation", Psalm cxlix. 4. Also, the thick foliage will afford shelter to many a weary traveller. Ideally, and prophetically, and we, too, in our degree, are in Isaiah xxxii. 2, where "A man shall be as an hiding place from the wind . . . as rivers of water in a dry place, as the shadow of a great rock [shall we say, a great tree] in a weary land". Happy the man who becomes a shelterer of others from the heats and hazards of life. Furthermore, do you recall this, "that they might be called trees of righteousness, the planting of the Lord, that He might be glorified", Isaiah lxi. 3? It is from His planting that the tree's promise flows. I heard on the radio the other day that on inheriting a great estate in Ireland, Lord Kilbracken planted there hundreds and hundreds of trees. The Lord of Heaven is a supremely great tree-planter. Has He planted us? Then are we making progress, "rooted in Him"? By the way, what a difference soil makes to growth. And don't forget to tend those roots. I lived in a certain vicarage for fifteen years which had a pear tree in the garden; but never a respectable pear did it yield me all that time. I am no gardener; but my successor was—and, strange to relate, he had a bumper crop his very first year. Why? He went at the roots, which I was too ignorant to do. That's it: take care of the roots, the secret connection with the Soil— the Quiet Time with GOD, and the use of His appointed means of grace—the Word; the Footstool; the Table; the Worship; the Work, "that ye may grow thereby", 1 Peter ii. 2, and "that He might be glorified": not we, but He. May we not be stunted trees.

Good buildings, 7. Speaking humanly, Paul exhausts his very considerable powers of metaphor to indicate the variety, vitality, and virility of the Christian life; and here is one more figure: the believer is to be as a building. *The Foundation*—"built up in Him". What a difference foundation makes to a house, as is so plainly illustrated in the

Master's "let's pretend" story of the two houses in Matthew vii. 24–7. The Sand House may very well have been just as attractive, just as comfortable, as Rock House: the trouble was that it was ill-founded, and so ill-fated when the storm broke. *The Fashion*—the happy style of the building in our passage is fairly deduced from the words here, "abounding therein with thanksgiving". Gladness opens the door of welcome, as if the mouth should utter a shout of praise. Joy streams out of the windows, as if the eyes shone to betray the grateful spirit within. Yes, the Christian may be, should be, as a building happy in the presence of its true Lord. Of a certain dwelling it was once said, "It was noised that He was in the house", Mark ii. 1. May it ever be so with the building of our lives. *The Finish*—of that building is not here indicated; but may it not be inferred from the statement that this person is "stablished in the faith"? For He Himself has laid the foundation—indeed, is Himself the Foundation Stone—"To whom coming, as unto a living stone . . . ye also, as living stones, are built up a spiritual house", 1 Peter ii. 4–5. But what of the hypothetical person of whom the Master sadly records, "This man began to build, and was not able to finish", Luke xiv. 30? The substructure was well and truly laid; but the superstructure never materialised. We should call him now a backslider, the object only of pity; oh yes, also of prayer. May any such be quickly restored, after the old promise of GOD, "I will heal their backsliding", Hosea·xiv. 4. And after the backsliding may they return to the upbuilding again: this time to a truly happy finish. So, then, here is advance, progress, in all directions—in knowledge, in life, in fruit, in character. And now—

WHAT WE SHOULD BEWARE

"*Enticing words,*" 4—persuasive speech. The apostle is far removed from those Christians in body; but he is right

alongside them in spirit. He is well aware of the danger
lurking in their midst, and of the insidious nature of the
enemy propaganda. We observe his anxiety for them, lest
by these specious approaches they should be "beguiled"
away from the truth. We observe, however, his joy that
they have thus far stood firm, "joying and beholding your
order and stedfastness of your faith in CHRIST". It is a
military figure that he uses: they have maintained a solid
front in the face of the "enticing words" of the enemy
agents. What a lure such speech can be in the undermining
of the unwary, either by the soft speech of the heretical
protagonist, or by the books they try to sell on your doorstep. One of the difficulties that some Christians have in
meeting these approaches is that the literature contains
so much of the Bible. Of course it does; Christian people
would not listen otherwise. That is how they are caught.
But we recall Shakespeare's sage remark, that "the devil
can quote Scripture to his purpose". But he then over-
reaches himself, by misquotation and misapplication, as his
effort in our Lord's temptation shews, if we compare
Matthew iv. 6 with Psalm xci. 11–12. Of Satan's emissaries
the Psalmist says, "every day they wrest my words", Psalm
lvi. 5. Does not the Lord speak through him? Indeed,
Peter, in speaking of Paul's Epistles, says, "in which are
some things hard to be understood, which they that are
unlearned and unstable wrest, as they do also the other
Scriptures, unto their own destruction", 2 Peter iii. 16.
That is just what these folk do: they wrest the Scriptures
—wrest them out of their context, and so wrest them out
of their meaning. By the way, the first thing to do with
these doorstep hawkers is to challenge them on 1 John
iv. 2–3, "Hereby know ye the SPIRIT of GOD: every spirit
that confesseth that JESUS is CHRIST come in the flesh is
of GOD; and every spirit that confesseth not . . . is not of
GOD". In other words, the prime test is the acknowledg-
ment of the full Deity of the incarnate Saviour. Not

enough that He be held to be a great teacher, or the best man ever—to grant Him anything less than absolute Deity is "anti-CHRIST". Start there, and you will soon be able to shut the door. But beware of their "enticing words".

"Philosophy and vain deceit," 8. We have a kindred warning where Paul is telling his protégé to avoid "oppositions of science falsely so called", 1 Timothy vi. 20. The apostle was a university-trained man, a great brain, and widely read, which is why he was able to attract an educated man like Dr. Luke, as well as those of a humbler sort. He would be the last man to decry the importance and value of philosophy and science as such. It is only their vagaries away from the truth that he is tilting against, and warning of. A science that forgets that its realm is ever advancing, and therefore is not unchanging, is "falsely so called"; but, on the other hand, how vastly true science has contributed to our comprehension of our world, and to our conception of the might and majesty of our GOD. Let not us Evangelicals be afraid of science truly so called. In the long run, and in increasing measure, it will not prove in conflict with the revelation of the Scriptures, but will, rather, confirm the same. As for philosophy, there is a kind, an atheistic school, that leaves GOD out of its reckoning, and is therefore a "vain deceit", since it leaves Him out who is the Chief Factor in the Argument. Rather shall GOD have the central place in our thinking, after the pattern of John Milton's philosophy, as in his *Paradise Lost,*

> "SPIRIT of GOD,
> What is dark in me illumine,
> What is low raise and support,
> That, to the height of this great argument,
> I may assert eternal providence,
> And justify the ways of GOD to men."

Be that your aim, your theme, O ye philosophers, and we will gladly and gratefully welcome your helping our thinking in the ways of truth. That other kind will only "spoil you", "make spoil of you", R.V., since it rules out all that is of GOD, and "after CHRIST", and confines itself exclusively to the teachings of men, "after the rudiments of the world"—stoicheia, the childish things, the A.B.C. of the world's "vain", empty, account of things. Beware, says the apostle, of being made captive ("spoil") by any such system of thought. The downgrading of GOD's creative activity, as taught by the Gnosticism of the time, against which this Epistle is, in part, written as an antidote, is a signal example of such puerile vanity. And now—

WHEN WE DO BELONG

The passage we have been studying has, in the main, a twofold theme—first, the progress we are expected to make, if we have begun in the Christian life; second, the dangers that inevitably lie in the pathway of that advance. In the two closing verses, 9–10, the HOLY SPIRIT leads Paul to make two statements which will assure our hearts of the possibility of that advance, and avoidance.

"*In Him dwelleth all the fulness of the Godhead bodily*," 9. That is eternally true, for He was, is, ever will be, in all respects, fully GOD. As the Athanasian Creed puts it— "The Godhead of the Father, of the Son, and of the Holy Ghost, is all one: the Glory equal, the Majesty co-eternal". In all the calls, the claims, and the consequences of the Christian life, we believers have to do with One who is fully GOD, and who is therefore fully capable of undertaking all our affairs and necessities. So this Paul is able to claim, "I can do all things [required of me] through CHRIST which strengtheneth me", Philippians iv. 13. What a comfort!

"*Ye are complete in Him*," 10. So fully and completely do we belong that the apostle, even in this brief passage, three times over refers to us as being "in Him". We might state the matter grammatically in the form of a syllogism—

(*a*) Fulness is in Him. (*b*) We are in Him. (*c*) Fulness is for us—not for us, of course, the fulness of Divine Godhead; but the fulness of Christian Manhood. That word "complete" is a picture word in the Greek. They tell me that it holds the idea of a ship fully rigged, and equipped, for the voyage. So is it applicable to the Christian voyaging forth on the ocean of life. "In Him"—is the *Captain*, in charge of the vessel; the *Chart*, of the Word, to be consulted daily; the *Compass*, of the conscience, regulated, educated by the Word; the *Commissariat*, food for the journey, from the stores of the Word; the *Crew*, of our fellow-travellers, working our passage, seeing that we have nothing with which to pay for the trip; the *Conquest*, of His indwelling presence and power, seeing that we are not as barges, having to be towed by others on the bank, nor are we as sailing ships, depending on the favourable winds of comfortable circumstance for our progress, but we are as liners, that have the power of their engines within to triumph over waves and storms. "CHRIST in you." The *Colour*, of our unashamed allegiance to Him to whom the ship belongs. Once the colour was the Skull and Crossbones of the rebel vessel; now it is the White Ensign, as a Flag-ship of the Divine Admiral of the Fleet. The *Coming into Port*—for "so He bringeth them unto their desired haven", Psalm cvii. 30. This is progress indeed, this is Full Salvation.

HIS WARNING OF SNARES

Warning of Snares

11 In whom also ye are circumcised with the circumcision made without hands, in putting off the body of the sins of the flesh by the circumcision of Christ:

12 Buried with him in baptism, wherein also ye are risen with *him* through the faith of the operation of God, who hath raised him from the dead.

13 And you, being dead in your sins and the uncircumcision of your flesh, hath he quickened together with him, having forgiven you all trespasses;

14 Blotting out the handwriting of ordinances that was against us, which was contrary to us, and took it out of the way, nailing it to his cross;

15 *And* having spoiled principalities and powers, he made a shew of them openly, triumphing over them in it.

16 Let no man therefore judge you in meat, or in drink, or in respect of an holyday, or of the new moon, or of the sabbath *days:*

17 Which are a shadow of things to come; but the body *is* of Christ.

18 Let no man beguile you of your reward in a voluntary humility and worshipping of angels, intruding into those things which he hath not seen, vainly puffed up by his fleshly mind,

19 And not holding the Head, from which all the body by joints and bands having nourishment ministered, and knit together, increaseth with the increase of God.

20 Wherefore if ye be dead with Christ from the rudiments of the world, why, as though living in the world, are ye subject to ordinances,

21 (Touch not; taste not; handle not;

22 Which all are to perish with the using;) after the commandments and doctrines of men?

23 Which things have indeed a shew of wisdom in will worship, and humility, and neglecting of the body; not in any honour to the satisfying of the flesh.

HIS WARNING OF SNARES
II. 11–23

YES, more warnings, for Paul, like a true pastor, is deeply
anxious about the safety and the welfare of the flock. It
appears, from the first verse of this chapter, that he had
not visited Colossæ, and that, therefore, these Christians
were not his children in the faith. I would think that
Epaphras, their founder and leader, i. 7, *was* one of Paul's
converts, and that these believers had, in the main, been
brought to CHRIST by him. If that be the case, then the
readers of this letter would be the apostle's grandchildren;
and he certainly displays here a grandfatherly concern for
their spiritual well-being. There is clear evidence here that
these Christians have grown "in grace, and in the knowledge of our Lord and Saviour JESUS CHRIST", 2 Peter
iii. 18. But false teaching is afoot; and it seems, as we
have said earlier, as if Epaphras has gone to Rome to discuss with Paul about it, and how to meet it. Our present
passage is a very difficult one; but we must try together to
grasp something of the drift of its arguments.

THE PITFALL OF JUDAISM, 11–17

The Old Covenant and the New—is the alternative theme
of verses 11–12. The controversy seems to have dogged·
Paul's footsteps almost everywhere he went. It was a
widespread view of these teachers that no Gentile could
become a Christian except via Judaism—he must, therefore, submit to the law of circumcision, the outward sign
of covenant relationship with GOD. But, says the apostle,
with the coming of CHRIST a new covenant has been in-
augurated, wherein is a new outward sign of covenant
relationship, a new circumcision, not now of the flesh but

63

of the spirit, symbolised by the ordinance of baptism, in which is typified the recipient's identification with CHRIST in His burial in death, and resurrection to life—"I have been crucified with CHRIST; nevertheless I live", Galatians ii. 20. Are we, then, to take it that Paul was speaking disparagingly, even scornfully, of the Old Covenant? By no means.

The Shadow and the Substance—is the way he designates the contrast in verses 16–17. Under the Old Economy of Law there were rules and regulations which the godly man was expected to observe—foods and feasts were appointed of GOD for man's health and holiness. Under the New Economy of Grace, however, all is altered—even "the sabbath day" is, with Divine blessing, changed from the seventh to the first. No Gentile convert is to be "judged", condemned, because of non-compliance with these ancient requirements. We Christians "are not under law (Gk.) but under grace", Romans vi. 14. That doesn't mean that we may live lawlessly, with a licence to sin (verse 15); "GOD forbid", says the horrified apostle. No, indeed; but our conduct now has a new motive—not legal, but love. "Thou shalt do no murder" is not cancelled, but is controlled by a new spirit, "Thou shalt love thy neighbour". But, I ask again, does all this mean that the Old Order is to be despised? No, again—"which are a shadow of things to come", a Divinely directed fore-shadowing of the CHRIST Who was to be the Substance. All these ordinances pointed on to Him, and when He came as the complete fulfilment of them all, their purpose was fully served, and the old order changed, giving place to the new. "A shadow"—yes, but, don't forget, a GOD-appointed shadow. All those Levitical sacrifices and offerings did not originate with Moses, but only came through him, from GOD Himself, so we will not speak irreverently of them, but thankfully recall their substantive significance.

The Blessing in CHRIST—is, consequently, placed before us in verses 13–15. Through our union with Him in His dying, and His rising, "together with Him", we have, amongst many other blessings, the primary boon of the forgiveness of sins, for through "His cross", and "in it", He accomplished an open triumph over all the forces of evil. Note how Paul here describes "the great Transaction", as Philip Doddridge's hymn characterises it. Consider, then, "the handwriting of ordinances that was against us". Was this not the Ten Commandments, "written with the finger of GOD", Exodus xxxi. 18; Deuteronomy ix. 10? "Against us", because they convict and condemn us for having so gravely and so grievously broken them. There stands the Law: how did Love deal with the situation? "Took it out of the way, nailing it to His cross." When the Romans crucified a man, it was customary to write a card stating the nature of his crime, and to nail it to the upright of his cross, which is exactly what happened in the case of our Lord, whose "superscription of His accusation", Mark xv. 26, proclaimed that His crime was His claim to be "King of the Jews", as if setting Himself against Cæsar. The truer "title", as Paul tells, was that the Ten Words were nailed there, and that the condemnation was for the breaking of the whole gamut of GOD's commands—not that He had broken them, but we had, and He was suffering in our stead. "The Lord hath laid on Him the iniquity of us all", Isaiah liii. 6. And so, "he that believeth on Him is not condemned", John iii. 18; v. 24. Blessed assurance! Not in Judaism, except as a picture, but in JESUS is all our hope of Full Salvation.

THE PITFALL OF GNOSTICISM, 18

This comes next under consideration. We have already indicated some of its significance; but here Paul goes into more detail, and in a few graphic expressions he gives—

Some of its teachings. It was a curious mixture, and a crude bundle of strange fancies: but let our verse speak for itself. (*a*) "A voluntary humility", that is, feigned, not genuine. They put it on to put you off your guard. It is almost an obsequiousness; but don't you allow it to "beguile" you. (*b*) "Worshipping of angels"—that spurious line of descending intermediaries for the creating of the world, since they allege the evil of matter as such, and therefore GOD's holy inability to have any direct connection with its formation. How ludicrously contrasted to the Bible's simple revelation. (*c*) "Intruding into those things which he hath not seen"—the things unseen refer to the cult of the Mystery Religions which flourished then in those quarters. After a period of mystic preparation, one was ready to step into the secret. This "intruding" was the final step into the inner shrine, and one became an initiate. It was apparently thus that one became, as it were, a fully-fledged member of this Gnostic sect. (*d*) "Vainly puffed up by his fleshly mind"—we have already noted that their vaunted humility was feigned, for their own purpose. Here the real truth is out, for this phrase is intended to convey their intellectual pride, and snobbery. So much for their humility! Their very name Gnostic is the Greek gnosis, which means knowledge—"we know"! Well, well!

Some of its losses—may be mentioned. (*a*) It robs its devotees of that true humility which in Scripture after Scripture is seen to be of such high value in the eyes of GOD—for instance, "the ornament of a meek and quiet spirit, which is in the sight of GOD of great price", 1 Peter iii. 4. I often think, and sometimes say, that there is no limit to what GOD can do with us if only we are humble enough. Perhaps we may say that the key to this quality is "Not I, but CHRIST", Galatians ii. 20. (*b*) This queer teaching robs its adherents of the only Mediator, instead of the long procession of deteriorating go-betweens. The Christian truth is that "there is One Mediator between GOD and men, the man CHRIST JESUS", 1 Timothy ii. 5. GOD's approach to men is by that One, "GOD was in CHRIST reconciling the world unto Himself", 2 Corinthians v. 19.

Man's approach to GOD is by that One, "No man cometh unto the Father but by Me", John xiv. 6. What a tragedy to be deprived of all the benefits of His mediatorial office. (b) This odd doctrine negatives the revealed mystery, with all its accompanying "riches", as referred to in chapter 1, verse 27, of this Epistle. The fact is that Christianity is the one only true Mystery Religion—held hidden through the long years of preparation covered by the Old Testament till men of faith, Gentile as well as Jew, were invited by GOD to take the step of initiation into the glorious company of the blessed Inheritors of the Open Secret, part of whose "riches" is the deeply moving truth that CHRIST did not merely come down to die for you, but comes to dwell in human hearts that invite Him in—"CHRIST in you, the hope of glory", Colossians i. 27. All this the peculiar Gnostics miss. For us who are believers, this golden mystery holds all the secret of Full Salvation.

THE PITFALL OF ASCETICISM, 20–3

A variation of Gnosticism. There were features common to both, but the most significant difference here was the emphasis upon the denial of the body; yet even this springs from the notion of the innate evil of matter. (a) This is a religion of don't—"touch not, taste not, handle not", 21. It reminds me of a small boy who, when asked his name, said that it was "Don't". When told he had misunderstood the enquiry, he insisted that he had told them his right name. "Whatever I do it is always Don't, Don't, Don't; yes, my name is Don't". Poor child; and poor religionist, whose life is circumscribed by an eternal Don't. Oh, for the positive delights of the Christian life—a bliss of which the ascetics were bereft. (b) It was characterised by a pseudo-wisdom—"a shew of wisdom". They fancied themselves, yet, for one thing, how unwise was their neglect of the body. Do you think we Christians are careful enough of our physical well-being? Should we not heed the reminder that "your body is the temple of the HOLY GHOST", 1 Corinthians vi. 19? Ought we not, by sensible feeding, by due cleansing, and by proper exercise, seek—so far as we may—to keep our body fit for any demands He may make of us for His service? Beware of the slick remark that it is better to wear out than to rust out. Yes, I am sure of that; but I am still more sure that it is better still to last out. How unwise it is to be "neglecting the body". (c) It exalts its own will—"in will worship", thinking by the exercise of strong will-power to attain to the perfection desired; but it is not, in any sense, a godly will, but is of "the flesh", that is, the lower carnal nature, which, says Paul, is ever "lusting against the SPIRIT", Galatians v. 17. Neither the new birth, nor any resulting blessing, is attainable "of the will of the flesh, nor of the will of man", John i. 13. Oh, for the worship of the will of GOD—

> "Thy wonderful grand will, my GOD,
> With triumph now I make it mine;
> And faith shall cry a joyous Yes
> To every dear command of Thine."

But what of the result of this cult of asceticism, does it work for goodness?

A complete failure. It is "not in any honour to the satisfying of the flesh". The Revised Version illuminates the meaning of this difficult phrase, which it renders, "not of any value against the indulgence of the flesh". A spiritual malady cannot be cured by a physical remedy. So, as we leave this passage, we remark on—

THE PITY OF IT ALL

In verse 20, the apostle asks, almost pathetically, "Wherefore if ye be dead with CHRIST . . . are ye subject to ordinances?" That is, if you really and truly are Christians, why ever allow yourselves to be misled and tied up with all these rules and regulations, whether emanating from

Judaism, or from Gnosticism, or from Asceticism? "Stand fast therefore in the liberty wherewith CHRIST hath made us free, and be not entangled again with the yoke of bondage", he would say, as in Galatians v. 1. *In verse* 19, he has put his finger on the reason why any such defection should ever take place, "not holding the Head"—not holding to the headship of the Head. We all know, if we allowed this in the physical frame, what dreadful consequences would accrue among the limbs of the body. Paul uses these material facts as similes of spiritual truths, as he has done already with such effect in 1 Corinthians xii.

The Source of our Service—"all the body by joints and bands . . . knit together". When all the parts are in right position, and healthy condition, the brain is able to direct the body in its various functions, and to regulate the service that it is intended to render. The thing holds good in the spiritual sphere. Let us see to it that there shall be no dislocation of the soul's "joints", no slipped discs of the heart—that there shall be no shrinking of the soul's "bands", the spiritual sinews, and moral muscles. So shall we make sure that the Head shall not be impeded in His strategic work in us, and through us, in service.

The Spring of our Health—"having nourishment ministered". Here once more is the brain at work for the well-being of the body, knowing how to control the nutriment supplied, and to turn it into life-force for the whole frame. Take one New Testament instance of the remarkable way in which the Head ministers to the nourishment of the soul. Two debilitated men, their spiritual vitality undermined by grief, are dragging their feet along the road to their village home. Presently we find them on the same road; but what has happened that this time, with hurrying footsteps, and uplifted spirits, they hasten back to Jerusalem? Simply that the Head has ministered the nourishment that has renewed their spirit and energy: by the Word— "did not our heart burn within us . . . while He opened to

us the Scriptures?" Luke xxiv. 32; and by the Sacrament—
"He was known of them in breaking of bread", verse 35.
In His Word, and at His Table, and through other means
of grace, He is ever wont to bring strength to our spiritual
being—strength for service, strength for health, and further—

The Secret of our Growth—"increaseth with the increase
of GOD". Our bodies will not grow big and strong if we
do not faithfully follow the dictates of the brain. Perhaps
our apostle has observed that some of these Colossian
Christians are shewing signs of developing into poor-
hearted, small-minded, weak-kneed, flabby-muscled, thin-
bodied, lame-limbed believers—all because, not holding to
the Head, they have suffered their strength to be sapped
by some insidious heresy. How different from the thrilling
summons of Isaiah xxxv. 3–4, "Strengthen ye the weak
hands, confirm the feeble knees. Say to them that are of
a fearful heart, Be strong, fear not: behold, your GOD. . . ."
Here is the fine, adventurous virility of the healthy, godly
life. Be it noted, then, that spiritual invalidism results
from "not holding the Head"; but that spiritual invigora-
tion comes from "beholding your GOD". "They that wait
upon the Lord shall renew their strength," Isaiah xl. 31.
What a pity it is that any of us Christians should, through
the enervating atmosphere of any heretical belief, allow
ourselves to sink into spiritual mediocrity, when we might
be enjoying the vigours of GOD's full salvation.

> "Love's resistless current sweeping
> All the regions deep within;
> Thought, and wish, and senses keeping
> Now, and every instant, clean:
>   Full salvation!
> From the guilt and power of sin."

HIS ENCOURAGEMENT OF AMBITION

COLOSSIANS III. 1–4

Encouragement of Ambition

1 If ye then be risen with Christ, seek those things which are above, where Christ sitteth on the right hand of God.

2 Set your affection on things above, not on things on the earth.

3 For ye are dead, and your life is hid with Christ in God.

4 When Christ, *who is* our life, shall appear, then shall ye also appear with him in glory.

HIS ENCOURAGEMENT OF AMBITION
III. 1-4

IT IS very evident that life for the Christian is intended to be very different from that of the worldling—different in nature, different in outlook, different in interests, different in aim. His rightful ambition is indicated in our present passage. It is described here as a resurrection life—"If ye then be risen with CHRIST", 1; and in Philippians iii. 10 it is perfected in "the power of His resurrection". See first—

THE CERTAINTY OF IT

"If", says our Authorised Version; "if", says ii. 20. But the Greek construction will not allow any such dubiety in these two fundamental matters. Moffatt's rendering gives us the true nature of the case. In chapter ii, he translates the original, given as "If ye be dead with CHRIST", by the words, "As you died with CHRIST". There is no doubt attached to it. In chapter iii here, it is not, "If ye then be risen with CHRIST", but as the Professor has it, "Since, then, you have been raised with CHRIST". There is no doubt about it. The apostle is writing to these people as Christians; and of all such it is indubitably true that these two basic certitudes abide. In view of their union with CHRIST, thank GOD, they are dead men; and, praise GOD, they are risen men. There is no "if" about either case, but the consequential "as", and "since".

But what is this "union with CHRIST" that we speak of? It results from an exercise of Identification by Faith. We go, for elucidation, away back to Leviticus i. 4, "He shall put his hand upon the head of the burnt offering, and it shall be accepted for him to make atonement for him". The same transaction is in iv. 24. Under the Old Covenant, to which we have already referred in these Studies, GOD made special arrangements for the temporary dealing with men's sins until the time came when it would be possible to deal with them permanently and eternally. "For it is not possible that the blood of bulls and of goats should *take away* sins," Hebrews x. 4—those sacrifices were ordained to cover sins (hence, "Blessed is he whose transgression is forgiven, whose sin is covered", Psalm xxxii. 1. That is as far as the Psalmist could go), until "now once in the end of the age hath He appeared to *put away* sin by the sacrifice of Himself", Hebrews ix. 26. Those oft-repeated offerings of the Old Testament pointed on to, and drew their significance from, the once-for-all Sacrifice of CHRIST in the New Testament. We shall meet those Old Testament believers on exactly the same ground. We believers will be there—the Cross of Calvary. "That by means of [His] death, for the redemption of the transgressions that were under the first testament", as Hebrews ix. 15 has it. Or, as in Romans iii. 25, "Whom GOD hath set forth to be a propitiation through faith in His Blood, to declare His righteousness for the remission of sins that are past, through the forbearance of GOD".

Well now, to come back to Leviticus. By Divine appointment the transgressor brought his animal victim as his offering for sin. The priest will have most carefully scrutinised the beast, to make sure that there was no spot or blemish. The offerer would now stand, and, placing his hand upon its head, confess his sin. In that moment the Great Transference would take place. GOD reckoned as if the sin of the man were laid on the beast, and the spotlessness of the animal accounted to him. The victim is then put to death as bearing the man's sin, and suffering in his stead. He left the scene a forgiven man. It was all a GOD-given, GOD-ordained, prophetic picture of what was afterwards to be; and old Isaac Watts has captured its significance for us in his great hymn—

> "My faith would lay her hand
>   On that dear head of Thine,
> While like a penitent I stand,
>   And there confess my sin."

Thus, by this heavenly Identification by Faith, we are joined to Him as ourselves dead to sin, and, moreover, as being alive in resurrection to "newness of life", Romans vi. 4, 11. This, be it ever remembered, not for any merit of ours, and quite independently of our understanding. Christian, as a matter of complete certainty, you are risen with CHRIST. The only question—for you and me—is whether we are living up to our high privilege, whether walking after "the power of His resurrection". Let us go on to another aspect of this truth.

THE CENTRE OF IT

Notice these phrases in our brief verses. "With CHRIST", 1; "where CHRIST", 1; "with CHRIST", 3; "when CHRIST", 4. It is pretty evident, isn't it, where the centre of the resurrection life lies. When all our life revolves around Him as our Living Centre, then we know resurrection life in happy truth. This indeed is Full Salvation. Mark here three statements that have an intimate bearing upon our relationship with Him.

"CHRIST *sitteth on the right hand of* GOD," 1. The Epistle to the Hebrews shews us that three things are implied in this posture of the Master. (1) *Rest*—"when He had by Himself purged our sins, sat down on the right hand of the Majesty on high", Hebrews i. 3. In amazing grace, He undertook the plan of our salvation, till, on its completion, He was able to say, "It is finished", John xix. 30. He undertook to pay in full the enormous debt of our sin, till, on its complete cancellation, He was free to say, "It is finished". The Cross was the payment in full; the Resurrection was GOD's receipt. He undertook, at the Father's will, to drink our cup of woe, till, on His drinking to the last bitter dregs, He handed back the cup to the Father, and said "It is finished". The plan that He came to earth to accomplish is now fully carried out, and He has gone back to Heaven to take His seat of rest at GOD's right hand. (2) *Intercession*—"seeing He ever liveth to make intercession for them", Hebrews vii. 25. Can we ever assess what we owe to our Saviour's prayers? Why, after his base denial, did not Peter fall away entirely? Listen: "I have prayed for thee, that thy faith fail not [utterly]", Luke xxii. 32. If anyone be so ill and weak that they cannot pray for themselves; or, if anyone be so lonely that there is no one they can ask to pray for them, what a deep comfort, in each case, to know that JESUS is there to pray for them. We say again that down here we shall never be able to estimate what we owe to His prayers for us. On one occasion, He looked into a house, and said of a man there, "Behold, he prayeth", Acts ix. 11. When we are in need of comfort and strength, may we not look into heaven, and say, "Behold, *He* prayeth"? (3) *Sovereignty*—"we see JESUS . . . crowned", Hebrews ii. 9. One day He is going to return to this earth to assume the Kingdom, which, on His present rejection, is in abeyance, when "the kingdoms of this world are become the kingdoms of our Lord and of His CHRIST, and He shall reign for ever and ever", Revelation xi. 15. But even now He reigns on high; and by reason of our union with Him, we, too, are entitled to reign with Him—in that one day of His millennial glory, "they shall reign with Him a thousand years", Revelation xx. 6, "we shall reign on the earth", Revelation v. 10, yes; but even now He "hath made us kings and priests", Revelation i. 6, in our degree to share in His present Sovereignty, and in His present Intercession. If only we would put into practical daily use our exalted position in Him!

"*Your life is hid with* CHRIST *in* GOD," 3. Who, then, will say that our life, once hid, can ever be lost? The Son and the Father are pledged to its security—"I give unto them eternal life, and they shall never perish, neither shall anyone pluck them out of My hand. My Father which gave them Me is greater than all, and no one is able to pluck them out of My Father's hand", John x. 28-9. "With CHRIST, in GOD"—what blessed safety: hidden as treasure deposited in a bank, the impregnable vaults of the Bank of Heaven, Matthew vi. 20; hidden as a root planted in a fertile soil, to bring forth the rich fruit of good seed, Matthew xiii. 38a. Incidentally, how important it is that we should cultivate the hidden life. The harvest of the fruit depends so much on the health of the root. Earlier in these Studies I have told the story of the pear tree from which I got practically nothing for fifteen years—"nothing but leaves", Mark xi. 13. The very first year of his occupancy, and ever after my successor had an abundant crop —the simple secret was that he treated the roots of the tree. Even the old prophet knew that way to the spiritual welfare of a nation, let alone to the life of an individual —"the remnant that is escaped of the house of Judah shall again take root downward, and bear fruit upward", Isaiah xxxvii. 31. So, to be hidden in Him is to be fruitful for Him, as well as to be safe, in His keeping power.

"CHRIST *who is our life,*" 4. Not only brings, or gives, but "is", in Himself. (1) *Its Entrance*—"He that hath the Son hath [the] life; he that hath not the Son of GOD hath not [the] life", 1 John v. 12. This latter has a physical life; but he has not "the" (Gk.) life, the spiritual life. He is our life. (2) *Its Continuance*—"I give unto them eternal life", John x. 28. Being eternal it continues: it lasts because He lasts. (3) *Its Abundance*—"I am come that they might have life, and that they might have it more abundantly", John x. 10. There is a world of difference between the two qualities. The hospital patient in that bed, only just alive—like some Christians, who, while having life, because they have Him, are only just Christians, they haven't grown. The hospital nurse bustling about the ward, full of life—that is the kind of Christian we are meant to be. (4) *Its Influence*— "By reason of him [Lazarus] many . . . believed on JESUS", John xii. 11. His new life, because of the Saviour, made this man a real advertisement for the Master, and enabled him to wield a powerful influence for Him on others. (5) *Its Fragrance*—"He could not be hid", Mark vii. 24. If He be in our heart and life in any effective degree, the fact is sure to be noticed. A friend of mine speaks of having met one day a lot of girls emerging from a factory for their lunch break. He says that they carried a most attractive aroma. As he then passed the gate he saw that it was a scent factory. Just so is it that if our life is "hid" in Him, something of His fragrance will be upon us—"the savour of life", 2 Corinthians ii. 16 calls it. I fancy it is true that fragrance comes from sacrifice. Anyhow, that was so when "the house was filled with the odour of the ointment", John xii. 3. When the box was broken, the fragrance was released. Certainly it is true that when the self is broken, the savour of CHRIST is known—"not I, but CHRIST", Galatians ii. 20. Well, all this that we have been saying is to emphasize the blessed truth that CHRIST Himself is the Living Centre of the resurrection life. Is He, then, the real centre of our life? We are all aware of the teachings of old astronomers concerning our planetary universe. Ptolemy was the first in the field (A.D. 127–51), one of the most eminent of the scientific men of the ancient world. He taught that our earth was the centre of the universe, and that all else revolved around it. How grand to think of ourselves as the hub of the universe! It took something like thirteen hundred years to dispel the illusion. Copernicus (A.D. 1473–1543) demonstrated that the sun was the centre, with the earth and all else revolving around it. I wonder if we have changed our life's centre? Because we begin by giving self that position—everything turns round ourselves: what we wish, we think, we propose. It often takes a long time for us to see the falsity, and futility, of the idea that this self, this bit of earth is the hub. It is a happy moment when we alter the outlook, and recognise "the Sun of Righteousness", Malachi iv. 2, as our new Centre. Thenceforward, every aspect of life rotates round Him. Such, then, is the resurrection life of Full Salvation. Now consider—

THE CIRCUMFERENCE OF IT

This resurrection life, centred in Him, not being self-centred, has a magnificent wide sweep. The risen life will never forget that while "He is the propitiation for our sins", it is "not for ours only, but also for the sins of the whole world", 1 John ii. 2. Do you know that story of a great Salvation Army conference that met in America a number of years ago, attended by delegates from all over the world? All were thrilled when they knew that the Old General himself was to be there. Near the date, however, his doctors forbade him to travel; but he promised to send a cable to open the conference. When the time came, there was anxiety in the assembly, for the message hadn't arrived; but then, just in the nick of time, it was brought. It consisted of one word—"Others". What a start, what a theme, for any Christian conference. How like the Saviour, of whom even His enemies had to acknowledge that "He saved others, not Himself", Matthew xxvii. 42. So it is that if He be our Centre, others will be our Circumference— "the whole world" of others, whom we may be able, by our prayers, our example, our testimony, to reach, to touch, and to fetch for Him. To that end—

"Set your affection"—rightly, for what we love we become like; and it is that likeness to Him that is destined to wield our greatest influence on others. But do you notice that the A.V. margin renders this "set your mind", and it suggests the idea of setting our watch by the sun? Our clock may be fast or slow, or may even have stopped, and

so we seek to put it right. It is not wise to make a guess, nor to follow other people's clocks; but the best way is to regulate it by Greenwich Mean Time, which ultimately means the sun. Yes, again, "the Sun of Righteousness", Malachi iv. 2. If we want to keep our lives right, let us regularly regulate them by Him. Thus, if those others want to know the right time from us, we shall not lead them astray since we ourselves are right with Him—"ye became followers of us, and of the Lord", 1 Thessalonians i. 6: Paul and his Lord blessedly synchronised, so that to go by him was tantamount to going by Him. May our behaviour be always so accurately adjusted that "we have the mind of CHRIST", 1 Corinthians ii. 16. So, then, set your mind—

"*Not on things on the earth.*" There are those "who mind earthly things", Philippians iii. 19. Strange as it may seem, some Christians are thus regulated. They just seem unable to rise above their conditions and circumstances— no resurrection life for them. Christians they are, but so low-level Christians, so incongruously dwelling all the time in the earthlies. One thinks of the occasion when a company of Israelites were forgathered with the Philistines, before a battle, when the princes of the latter asked, in surprise, "What do these Hebrews here?" 1 Samuel xxix. 3. One is inclined to ask concerning believers who are earth-bound, "What do these Christians here?" Of course, we cannot ignore earthly things. When we became Christians, we were not at once transported to heaven, but left here to be a "*Salt*" of the earth, to stave off corruption, to be a "*Light*" of the world, to illumine the darkness, to be a "*City*" set on a hill, to guide people on to the city "whose builder and maker is GOD", Hebrews xi. 10. These three ministries are committed to us as part of the economy of the Kingdom, Matthew v. 13–14. Yes, indeed, "in the world", but not "of the world", John xvii. 11, 16.

"*On things above.*" There are the things which are to

guide our life below. We are to accumulate *Possessions in Heaven*—"lay up for yourselves treasures in heaven, where neither moth nor rust doth corrupt, and where thieves do not break through nor steal", Matthew vi. 20. So different from earth's treasures. We are to value *Popularity with Heaven*—it is said of some that "they loved the praise of men more than the praise of God", John xii. 43. How different is Paul's good soldier, "that he may please Him who hath chosen him to be a soldier", 2 Timothy ii. 4. We are to enjoy e'en here the *Pleasures of Heaven*—"in Thy presence is fulness of joy, at Thy right hand there are pleasures for evermore", Psalm xvi. 11. So different from "the pleasures of sin for a season", Hebrews xi. 25. We are to rejoice in a *Position in Heaven*—"but rather rejoice because your names are written in heaven", Luke x. 20. So different from those, however great and famous they may be, who are only "written in the earth", Jeremiah xvii. 13. We are to endure and energize for the *Prize of Heaven*—"forgetting those things which are behind, and reaching forth unto those things which are before, I press toward the mark for the prize of the high ["upward", Gk.] calling of GOD in CHRIST JESUS", Philippians iii. 13–14. So different from the "corruptible crown", 1 Corinthians ix. 25, which is the best that earth's striving can attain. We are to covet the *Power of Heaven*—"tarry ye . . . until ye be endued with power from on high", Luke xxiv. 49. So different from man, who out of much failure has to confess "How frail I am", Psalm xxxix. 4. Assuredly, it is our wisdom to set our minds thus "on things above". Such is the outlook of the resurrection life, always the uplook: to speak metaphorically, their habit is "Look from the top", Song of Solomon iv. 8. And now, to conclude, look at—

THE CIRCLE OF IT

"*When* CHRIST, *who is our life, shall appear, then shall ye also appear with Him in glory.*" So the fact of our union with CHRIST, through the Identification by Faith, has now come round full circle—we died in Him, we were buried with Him, we have been raised with Him, we are ascended with Him, we are seated with Him, we now anticipate the time when we shall return and reign with Him. Such is the glorious teaching of all these Pauline Letters—Romans, Galatians, Ephesians, Colossians. Thus we observe the Resurrection Life—from the root, in the Cross, to the Fruit, in the Coming. This is Full Salvation.

> Life immortal, heaven descending,
> Lo! my heart the SPIRIT'S shrine:
> GOD and man in oneness blending,
> Oh, what fellowship is mine!
>   Full salvation!
> Raised in CHRIST to life divine!

HIS GUIDANCE ON GARMENTS

Guidance on Garments

5 Mortify therefore your members which are upon the earth; fornication, uncleanness, inordinate affection, evil concupiscence, and covetousness, which is idolatry:

6 For which things' sake the wrath of God cometh on the children of disobedience:

7 In the which ye also walked some time, when ye lived in them.

8 But now ye also put off all these; anger, wrath, malice, blasphemy, filthy communication out of your mouth.

9 Lie not one to another, seeing that ye have put off the old man with his deeds;

10 And have put on the new *man,* which is renewed in knowledge after the image of him that created him:

11 Where there is neither Greek nor Jew, circumcision nor uncircumcision, Barbarian, Scythian, bond *nor* free: but Christ *is* all, and in all.

12 Put on therefore, as the elect of God, holy and beloved, bowels of mercies, kindness, humbleness of mind, meekness, longsuffering;

13 Forbearing one another, and forgiving one another, if any man have a quarrel against any: even as Christ forgave you, so also *do* ye.

14 And above all these things *put on* charity, which is the bond of perfectness.

HIS GUIDANCE ON GARMENTS

III. 5–14

IF YOU are a soldier, you must dress the part; if you are a cricketer, you must dress the part; if you are a bus driver, you must dress the part; if you are a Christian, you must dress the part. The resurrection life demands a complete change of costume. What a practical person is this inspired correspondent. He deals in his letters with the highest of themes; but it is never long before he brings them down to the level of the workaday life, and shews how the heavenly doctrine is intimately related to the homely details of everyday living. Think, for instance, of that great teaching on full surrender, in Romans xii. 1–2, and mark how at once, from verse 3 onward, he applies it all to the common round. See, too, in the Epistle to the Ephesians, how in the first part he is in the Heavenlies, and in the closing chapters he is in the Homelies, speaking of the mutual obligations of wives and husbands, of children and parents, of servants and masters. Like the apostle John, he regards the truth, not merely as something to be held, or to be admired, or to be taught, but as something we are to "do", 1 John i. 6. Doctrine is always linked with Doing. Paul pursues this same habit here in Colossians. "Habit"—why, the French use that word to describe clothes—a habit may refer to a coat, a skirt, a suit. It is interesting to observe how often Paul speaks of our personal habits and characteristics under the illustration of clothes. He does so in our present passage.

THE WARDROBE OF THE SOUL

The Old Clothes—first claim our attention. (*a*) What they are—truly a lot of junk, and worse. Look at the moth-eaten garments in verse 5, and that other list of disreputable pieces of apparel in verses 8–9. Do you notice that, in the latter list, so many iniquities are those of the mouth? What a power speech is for good will—a bit for control, a helm for guidance, in the one case; a fire, a beast, a poison, says James iii. 2–8. In the first list, it is interesting to note the phrase, "covetousness, which is idolatry". But do Christians worship idols? Yes, alas. The covetous man in the phrase has made an idol of some possession, some position, which he covets, and which, perchance, he will seek to secure by hook or by crook. (*b*) What GOD thinks of such clothes—"for which things' sake the wrath of GOD cometh on the children of disobedience", 6. All too often we play with sin, and trifle with GOD—we speak of our foibles, our weaknesses, our failures, when GOD calls them sins. We trade on His mercy, and forget the awful reality of His wrath. Our disobedience incurs His displeasure— and that is gravely serious. (*c*) What we all wore once— "in the which ye also walked some time, when ye lived in them", 7. Walking about in rags; for even if we were respectable citizens, in our own and in others' eyes, we were not so in GOD's eyes. He says concerning humanly-well-thought-of people, "all our righteousnesses are as filthy rags", Isaiah lxiv. 6. However well-dressed we were in a material sense, we were wholly unattractive in spiritual vesture. (*d*) What had we best do with these old clothes? "Put off all these", 8. Discard, and destroy them— "mortify", 5. They are fit for nothing but the rubbish bin and the furnace.

The New Clothes—now come under inspection. (*a*) What they are: a lovely list, as is to be seen in verses 12–14. (*b*) Why should they be worn—"as the elect of GOD". The elect should always be select. As we said earlier, if we are Christians we should dress the part. A believer who is spiritually down-at-heels, and out-at-elbows, is a disgrace to his profession; and he could be so well-turned-out. When, in our Lord's parable, the king punished the "man that had not on a wedding garment", Matthew xxii. 11, it was the fellow's own stupid fault, for the festive robe was offered at the entrance. Perhaps he said he could not afford one—but they were free to all the guests. Perhaps he thought his own clothes were good enough—but that did not satisfy the king. Perhaps he was late, and rushed in at the last moment—but he should have allowed nothing to hinder his coming to so important a function. Why I am quoting the incident here is because the right dress was available and he could have it for the receiving. So we will remember that all these wonderful qualities of Christian demeanour and behaviour can be ours. (c) What to do with them—"put on", 12. It is not enough to admire them, or to covet them. In another connection, when speaking of a Christian soldier's uniform and accoutrement, Paul says, "put on the whole armour of GOD", Ephesians vi. 11. So, then, as you seek to match the new life which you have "in CHRIST", two immensely important things await you—"put off", 8, and "put on", 10. (d) But, one moment: don't you like that overcoat—"above all these things put on love", 14. As we go out to face life, we shall often find it very chilly. Cold winds of opposition may come about us, to blow at our allegiance to CHRIST; dark clouds of disapproval may frown on our Christian stand for Him —don't let us go out without our overcoat. The love of GOD will warm our hearts and spirits. What matter the cold looks of men? The saintly Horatius Bonar says,

> "Men heed thee, love thee, praise thee not;
> The Master praises, what are men?"

We remind ourselves, too, that this very overcoating of the love of GOD—His for us, and ours for Him—will also kindle within our hearts a love for others, even for those who oppose themselves. So may people admire our overcoat, and seek to enquire where they can get one like it. And now for—

THE WEARER OF THE CLOTHES

A change of personality precedes a change of dress. It is useless to speak to non-Christians about all these Christian qualities. To expect them to wear such characteristics is like expecting young David to sally forth to meet Goliath in Saul's armour—"I cannot go with these", 1 Samuel xvii. 39.

"*Ye have put off the old man*," 9. This is not the old nature. Paul's name for that is "the flesh", the entail of Adam's fall, which is in every child of Adam, down through the human race, and which remains with us till the end of our days here below. We have our temptations from without—from the world, and the devil; and these are aggravated by temptation from within—this "flesh", acting like a spy in the castle, in league with the enemy without. If left undealt with, it will lead us far astray, wandering off in the ways of wickedness. The ancient game of bowls provides an excellent illustration of this working of "the flesh" within us. A little white ball—the "jack"— is trundled along to the other end of the green, and the player has to bowl his "wood" to lie as near to the jack as he can. It looks so easy, if you have a straight eye. But, try it and see. Inside your wooden ball is a piece of metal, a bias, which will cause it to go astray, in spite of your careful aim. The skill is in allowing for the bias, and thus counteracting it. Our old sinful nature, "the flesh" within, is destined to lead us astray, in collaboration with the temptations from without—"every man is tempted when he is drawn away of his own lust, and enticed", James i. 14. Thank GOD, there is a way of control. "The flesh lusteth [fighteth] against the SPIRIT, and the SPIRIT against the flesh," Galatians v. 17. The Christian has become a two-natured man : the abiding old nature wars for control, *but* [the Greek allows that for the "and", as the same original word is translated in verse 22] the indwelling new nature fights, too. The secret of conquest is to let the HOLY SPIRIT take over the conflict. But, we have ourselves been straying here. All this is about what the "old man" is not. What, then, is he? Very simply, the old man is the man of old—the person we used to be before our conversion. (a) *The old man's Decease*—"our old man is crucified with Him", Romans vi. 6, by the reckoning of GOD, through the Identification by Faith, of which we spoke at some length in our last chapter. (b) *The old man's Dress*—"ye have put off the old man with his deeds", Colossians iii. 9. His conduct is being likened here to his costume. (c) *The old man's Double*—"ye put off as concerning the former conversation [manner of life] the old man", Ephesians iv. 22, the way you used to go on in the old regenerate days. Alas, it sometimes happens that, because he is taken off his guard, a believer is betrayed into doing, or saying, something that was habitual in the old days, but which, at his New Birth, he has discarded, and for the moment he behaves like the old man's double. In such an event, if a Christian came down to breakfast in a temper, it wouldn't be a bad idea for his wife to rebuke him with the remark, "My dear, you've got the old man's waistcoat on this morning".

"*Ye have put on the new man,*" 10. That poor deformed savage Caliban, in Shakespeare's *Tempest,* spoke better than he knew when he said—

> "'Ban, 'Ban, Ca-Caliban
> Has a new master; get a new man."

When CHRIST is our Saviour and Master we have to put on the new man. May I remind you that "if any man be in CHRIST he is a new creature", 2 Corinthians v. 17? Being a Christian, he is to dress the part. "The garment of praise", says Isaiah lxi. 3; "He hath clothed me with the garments of salvation, He hath covered me with the robe of righteousness", verse 10 of the same chapter. Some sightseers, wandering about the grounds of a famous castle on an "open" day, came across an old man, evidently, by his old clothes, one of the gardeners, and they asked him, "Is the Duke in residence?"—It *was* the Duke! Just then he wasn't dressing the part. So far as the Christian uniform is concerned, the Christian soldier must never be in mufti. The story is told of the thorough-going conversion of an old disreputable blackguard, whose wife and children had been miserably beaten and bruised in his drunken brawls. Everyone in the town knew of old drunken John, unsavoury character that he was. On his conversion, he knew that everything must now be different—he thought of the way he had treated his family; he decided that he must leave his wretched hovel of a house, and find a decent home for them. On going to the agents, they made it plain to him that they were not going to entrust one of their respectable dwellings to an old reprobate like him. They knew old John. But his answer was, "I think you're making a mistake. I fancy you're confusing me with somebody else. Old John is dead; I'm new John". Well done! And now he is going to dress the part. It is so with all new-born people of GOD. Whether they are Greek folk, or Jewish, Barbarian, Scythian, slave or free (verse 11), they all dress alike. "CHRIST is all, and in all." This spiritual suiting is the height of fashion in the circles of Heaven, and the old clothes look so drab beside them. No wonder that Christians are exhorted, "As obedient children, not fashioning yourselves ·according to the former lusts in your ignorance", 1 Peter i. 14, when, not knowing any better, you thought yourselves looking very smart. And now one last thing—

THE WORTHINESS OF THE APPEARANCE

"*After the Image of Him that created him,*" 10. We have been talking about putting on various Christian virtues, and we have seen how becoming they are in a Christian; but now, in finishing this Study, we take the matter a step further. We, of course, recall that when GOD formed man, "in the Image of GOD created He him", Genesis i. 27; and now that we come to man's new creation in CHRIST, we learn that a like principle obtains—"after the Image of Him that created him" anew. This likeness to Him is, indeed, of the very purpose of our redemption—"for whom He did foreknow, He also did predestinate to be conformed to the Image of His Son", Romans viii. 29. May we not say, then, that GOD cares intensely to produce this Christ-likeness in His children. It is very moving to observe that He so often uses the untoward circumstances of our life to impress this pattern on believers' hearts and lives. Paul knew that so well, and he had suffered much. Listen to him: "We know that all things work together for good to them that love GOD," Romans viii. 28—we don't always think it, understand it, appreciate it, but "we know" it. Let an old patriarch say, in effect, the same thing, and he knew what he was talking about: "He knoweth the way that I take: when He hath tried me I shall come forth as gold," Job xxiii. 10. Even as I write these lines, I am thinking of a friend of mine in whom I have seen this very thing happen. A strong, healthy, vigorous, young sportsman—full of life, "full of beans". He was suddenly struck with crippling affliction. There has been no repining, no complaining. He has accepted it trustfully as in GOD's plan for him; but how remarkably his suffering has sweetened his disposition—"as gold", yes, indeed. And it is such a joy to see how he is triumphing over his disability. Let us listen to one further testimony, from the last of the prophets, "He shall sit as a refiner and purifier of silver", Malachi iii. 3—"sit", because the operation is a very delicate one; and the refiner will be satisfied with his work when he can see his face in the purified metal. One day we shall be perfectly "like Him", 1 John iii. 2, in an appearance of soul consonant with all His work for us, and in us. And in that day, wonder of wonders, "He shall

see of the travail of His soul, and shall be satisfied",
Isaiah liii. 11. And meanwhile—

"*As* CHRIST . . . *so* . . . *ye,*" 13. While we move amongst
others, it is GOD's plan for us that we should represent
Him to men. As the moon reflects the sun in yonder sky,
so are we to reflect "the Sun of Righteousness" on earth—
albeit, of necessity, a pale reflection. "As He is, so are we
in this world," 1 John iv. 17. If we are CHRIST's, we are
called upon to live what my friend, the late Dr. W. Y. Fuller-
ton, used to call "the Christly life". It is our exceeding
privilege, by the character of our demeanour and behaviour,
to remind people of Him. I shall never forget how this
was pressed upon my own conscience by a saying of a
little boy. Years ago I was leading the Children's Special
Service Mission at one of our South Coast holiday resorts.
As I was approaching the beach one morning, this little
fellow was going along there, too. As he caught sight
of me, he said, "Mummie, here comes the JESUS man".
He only meant that I was the man who spoke to the children
about the Saviour; but his remark meant far more to my
heart that day. What right had I—have I—to be called a
JESUS man? What degree of resemblance is there about
us? I wonder if you have read that moving story of
Jerome K. Jerome's called *The Passing of the Third Floor
Back*? Roughly, the tale is of a poor-class lodging house,
where lived a heterogeneous company of needy and seedy
folk, and where there was a poor, ignorant little servant-
girl, a good deal of a slut, and ready to sell her virtue for
a worthless trinket. Into the place there came one day a
lodger who at once seemed to be different, and who occu-
pied the third floor back. He quickly revealed himself to
have a very kind heart and way. He always had a kindly
word for the little slavey, usually so ignored and down-
trodden. She soon almost worshipped him. The other
lodgers, too, owed him much for his many deeds of helpfulness. He was always doing something for somebody, in

his kindly, sympathetic way. At last the day came for him to move elsewhere. The little maid watched him, open-eyed, as he walked with his bit of luggage to the front door; and as he turned to her with a smile and a gentle pat on the shoulder, she took her leave of him with the words, "Please, are you 'Im?" Is there any need to point the moral? The moving story was fiction. Could anything like it be fact in our lives? "Like Him." It is the HOLY SPIRIT alone who can do this for us, in us, 2 Corinthians iii. 18.

HIS IDEAL HOME EXHIBITION

Ideal Home Exhibition

15 And let the peace of God rule in your hearts, to the which also ye are called in one body; and be ye thankful.

16 Let the word of Christ dwell in you richly in all wisdom; teaching and admonishing one another in psalms and hymns and spiritual songs, singing with grace in your hearts to the Lord.

17 And whatsoever ye do in word or deed, *do* all in the name of the Lord Jesus, giving thanks to God and the Father by him.

18 Wives, submit yourselves unto your own husbands, as it is fit in the Lord.

19 Husbands, love *your* wives, and be not bitter against them.

20 Children, obey *your* parents in all things: for this is well pleasing unto the Lord.

21 Fathers, provoke not your children to *anger,* lest they be discouraged.

22 Servants, obey in all things *your* masters according to the flesh; not with eyeservice, as menpleasers; but in singleness of heart, fearing God:

23 And whatsoever ye do, do *it* heartily, as to the Lord, and not unto men;

24 Knowing that of the Lord ye shall receive the reward of the inheritance: for ye serve the Lord Christ.

25 But he that doeth wrong shall receive for the wrong which he hath done: and there is no respect of persons.

1 Masters, give unto *your* servants that which is just and equal; knowing that ye also have a Master in heaven.

HIS IDEAL HOME EXHIBITION

III. 15–IV. 1

AMONG the greatest achievements of Christianity is the Christian Home, which fact has so often created a deep impression on the mission field. It is important to note how great a stress the New Testament places on it. To take two instances. When Legion had been so gloriously transformed by the Lord JESUS, he wanted straightaway to go overseas for Him, to bear witness to His gracious power to heal and save; but the Master had other plans for him, "Go home . . . and tell them", Mark v. 19; "and shew . . ." Luke viii. 39. Home was to be his first mission field, as it is for all Christians. How strikingly successful this man was in his home ministry is seen in the fact that these people who had turned JESUS away, when He returned, "gladly received Him, for they were all waiting for Him", Luke viii. 40. Yes, if you have never yet done it, "tell" the news, and "shew" the new man at home. Extend the borders of your testimony afterwards; but, home first. One further instance of the same Christian principle, and order of things. Says Paul, "Learn first to shew piety at home", 1 Timothy v. 4. Here is one of the first lessons in the Primary School of the Christian life. We shall, of course, enlarge our circle of Christian behaviour as time goes on, and as opportunity occurs—but, home first. Alas, we have heard of some Christians who seem to have thought of their home as the place wherein there is no need to display the true spirit of CHRIST—it is often the most difficult place in which to do it, but let us ever bear in mind this "first" rule of the faith. And we will not forget that showing piety does not mean talking about religion, but living it. So we come to look at Paul's Ideal Home Exhibition.

The Members of the Household

Husband and wife, 18–19. This relationship is, of course, fundamental to the well-being of the home. Not a few children have developed disastrously simply because of the sad relationship existing between these two. Children notice far more than parents sometimes realise. How truly tragic it is when those who should be the home-makers become the home-breakers. God counts the family life as so deeply important, which, we may be sure, is why He "setteth the solitary in families", Psalm lxviii. 6. (1) *Wives* are given this guiding word, "submit", which does not imply a kind of abject slavery to the Great Man. Indeed, in the parallel passage in Ephesians, in the verse immediately before this exhortation to the ladies, the word occurs also in a wider application, "submitting yourselves one to another", Ephesians v. 21–2. I think we shall not go far wrong if we give to the expression the connotation of "mutual service". Each is to serve the highest interest of the other; and the women are reminded that, subject only to the overlordship of the Lord Himself, this is their proper attitude—"as it is fit in the Lord". In His concern for the welfare of the man, is it not a rather beautiful conception and name that God has for his wife—"I will make him an helpmeet for him", Genesis ii. 18? Happy the home when the wife "fits" into that Divine pattern. (2) *Husbands,* too, are given a guiding word, "love", which is also, of course, to be mutual. Perhaps, in the heathen atmosphere of Colossæ, in which these church members were bred, and were only lately emerged, men all too often regarded their wives as little more than chattels, and that is why Paul felt it necessary to emphasize, even to Christians, that love was to be the rule of the relationship, not harshness—accommodating, not demanding. Is anything more delightful than the obvious, mutual love of a married couple—and the sight of an old Darby and Joan who are quite evidently sweethearts still?

Parent and Child, 20–21. What a joy to have little people of your own; ay, and what a responsibility! I often think, when a child is given to mother and father, of GOD saying to them, "Take this child, and nurse it for me, and I will give thee thy wages", Exodus ii. 9. What wages of happiness, and pride, and love are yours if you find them growing up for GOD! (1) *Children* are given a guiding word, "obey", and that "in all things". The only restriction is, as in the Ephesian passage, "in the Lord"—one implication being that if the parent demanded something that would be wrong in the Lord's sight, the child is required to follow the higher loyalty. When Oliver Twist was being trained by old Fagin to pick pockets, he could have invoked a higher loyalty, and obeyed, rather, the Lord, who said, "Thou shalt not steal". The original word for children in our passage is not that for the "babes" of 1 Peter ii. 2, nor that for the "young children" of Mark x. 13, but a word implying one grown to years that could discern the clash of loyalties. But, with this one exception, he is still to obey his parents in all things. It is a delightful picture that we have of the twelve-year-old boy JESUS accompanying His mother and Joseph back from Jerusalem to the home at Nazareth, where He "was subject unto them", Luke ii. 51. One thinks, too, of the lovely upbringing of Tiny Tim, who "from a child [babe] hast known the Holy Scriptures", 2 Timothy iii. 15—reared on "the sincere [Gk. unadulterated] milk of the Word", 1 Peter ii. 2; and taught the faith by mother and grannie, 2 Timothy i. 5. What a grand household is here envisaged. Alas, that "disobedient to parents", 2 Timothy iii. 2, is an all-too-common feature of this present age. By the way, may I be so bold as to suggest that we are never too old to disregard the wishes of our parents—the relationship will no longer be the childlike "obey", but the "honour thy father and thy mother", Exodus xx. 12, endorsed by our Lord who originally gave it on Sinai, Luke xviii. 20. It is greatly distressing to observe the callous and grudging way in which some—yes, even some Christians—treat their obligation to care for the old folk, who in bygone years so lovingly cared for them. Shame on such unchristian behaviour! (2) *Fathers* also have a guiding word here, "provoke not". It is so easy to "discourage" the children by constant nagging at them, or by the use of the unfair method of heavy sarcasm, and what not. The reader will recall the little boy who said his name was "Don't". On it being supposed that he hadn't understood the question, he insisted, and explained, "Wherever I am, and whatever I'm doing, it's always, Don't, Don't, Don't. I'm right sick of it. That's my name, Don't". Poor little creature! And how much light is thrown on the life in the home when a mother sent her daughter upstairs with the instructions, "Go and see what Johnny is doing, and tell him not to". Talk about provoking children to anger! In some homes it is not surprising that the children are irritated and resentful. How different it can be when the child's parents seek, carefully and prayerfully, to "bring them up in the nurture and admonition of the Lord", Ephesians vi. 4.

Master and Servant, iii. 22–iv. 1. This latter word is a very mild and inadequate rendering of the original Greek, which indicates that the man was a slave—a bond-slave: the absolute property of the man who had bought him. It is the same word as Paul used so often when he described himself— as he delighted to do—as the "servant [bond-slave] of JESUS CHRIST", Romans i. 1. (1) *Servants* are given much sound advice here. Look at some of the phrases employed. (*a*) "Not with eyeservice": a homely illustration will make that clear. When asked how she knew she had become a Christian, a servant-maid said, "Because I sweep under the mats now". An excellent test! Some people's service is rendered in the spirit that "what the eye doesn't see, the heart won't grieve over". (*b*) "Whatsoever ye do, do it heartily, as to the Lord and not unto men." This is not spiritual work, but the ordinary work required in the home, or on the estate, of the slave owner. If the Lord were his earthly Owner, he wouldn't be slack about it. Let this Christian slave, then, do his work for his worldly master as if he were doing it for the Heavenly Master. Brother Lawrence could pursue "The Practice of the Presence of GOD" in his monastery kitchen. Do you remember what is said about Joseph? "The Lord was with Joseph . . . and his master saw that the Lord was with him", Genesis xxxix. 2–3. I suppose there was a fidelity about the way he did his work that impressed Potiphar. May we all do our ordinary daily work in a like spirit. (c) "Ye serve the Lord CHRIST". Samuel Chadwick used to say that he wrote his letters as if he were writing to the Lord, and so was careful that there should be no blots or mistake. What was that which one of our poets said about, "Who sweeps a room for the Lord's sake, makes that and th'action fine"?— I don't think I have got that right, but that was the sentiment. Mrs. C. F. Alexander has long taught our children to sing, "And still do all for JESUS' sake". A young assistant was minding the shop while the boss was out at lunch when a commercial traveller entered, and presently suggested some shady transaction. On seeing that the young fellow demurred, he said, "It's all right; after all, the master's not in". To which the youngster, with up-pointing finger, replied, "My Master is always in". That's it; let us pursue our earthly occupation as ever under His eye. (2) *Masters*, too, have their duties, toward their employees, to treat them justly and fairly. Is it not strange that this verse has got into the fourth chapter when it so obviously belongs to the third? Shall we dare to call it an archbishop's mistake? The fact is that it was not until the 13th century A.D. that the Bible was divided up into chapters. It was then done by Archbishop Stephen Langton (who, by the way, also supervised King John's signing of the Magna Charta—so we owe him a great debt), but His

Grace does seem to have slipped up here. Incidentally, the verse divisions waited another 300 years, and were eventually undertaken by a printer, Robert Stephens, not immaculately. But who are we to criticise such meticulous and immense labours, that have proved of such enormous assistance to us in our study of the Word. Well now, to return. The masters are ever to bear in mind that they "also have a Master in heaven", who, without "respect of persons", oversees them and their workmen alike—watching the way the man does his work, and the way the master treats him. Both are "under the Great Taskmaster's eye". Here, then, are the Divine directions that will make for the Ideal Home, in which all the members of the household co-operate toward this desirable end. It will now be quite natural to turn our particular attention to a consideration of—

THE HEAD OF THE HOUSE

Humanly speaking, indeed, Scripturally speaking, "the husband is the head", Ephesians v. 23, and where this order is duly observed it makes for the well-being of the family life. However, it sometimes happens that the wife usurps the man's rightful position and authority, and is patently and often aggressively in command. Except in unusual circumstances, that is not good. No reversal of GOD's appointed order, in any sphere, is good. The inspired apostle bases this precedence upon the fact that "Adam was first formed, then Eve", 1 Timothy ii. 13. Let him remain "first" in the house. Occasionally it is found that an old servant rules the roast; and, would you believe it, it has been known for a spoilt and pampered child to be the hub and pivot of the home life!

Note that, in our present passage, "the LORD" is mentioned by that name no less than seven times. The absolute lordship is His by blood-bought right—over "mind and mouth and members", as the late Bishop Taylor Smith

used to say; over heart and hands and homes; over everything. A university undergraduate had learned well who
wrote on the flyleaf of his Bible this couplet—

> "If you do not crown Him Lord of all
> You do not really crown Him Lord at all."

A life that is lived by this rule is one that knows the reality
of Full Salvation. Do you recall that printed card which
used often to be found hanging in the entrance hall of a
home—

> "CHRIST is the Head of this house,
> The unseen Guest at every meal,
> The silent Listener to every conversation."

It is, in essence, the same as the challenging testimony of
Joshua in his farewell address to the people whom he had
led into Canaan—"Choose you this day whom ye will
serve . . . as for me and my house, we will serve the Lord",
Joshua xxiv. 15. It reminds me of one of the loveliest
noises ever heard, "It was noised that He was in the
house", Mark ii. 1—and, attracted by that noise, how
many came and were blessed. Ay, blessed indeed, and
happy the domicile if He be the Head. We turn then to
discover for ourselves—

THE SECRETS OF THE HOME

The Peace, 15—"Let the peace of GOD rule in your
hearts". It is obviously GOD's plan that this quality should
flourish in companies, as well as in individuals—"in one
body" of people, whether, as here, in the body of the
family, or in the body of the fellowship, the church. How
saddened Paul was concerning the two ladies at logger-
heads in the Philippian church—"I beseech Euodias, and
beseech Syntyche, that they be of the same mind in the
Lord", Philippians iv. 2. Such a situation has before now
sapped the energy of a church community, and stopped
its blessing. And who can measure the loss and sadness

when members of the same home are scarcely on speaking terms. How "thankful" we should be when a peaceful spirit prevails. Look for a moment at that word "rule". Its significance really is "arbitrate". John Milton calls conscience "the umpire of the soul"; but here, in "the peace of GOD", is an infallible referee for the spirit. Does that line of conduct disturb our peace? That thing I want to do, that place I want to visit, that letter I want to write, that circle I want to join—does it becloud the sun of His peace? If it does, Don't! It is a first-rate test for a first-rate Christian. It is grand to have "the peace of GOD" in our hearts; it is surpassing grand to have "the GOD of peace" there, in full control—of circumstances, and of conduct, Philippians iv. 7, 9.

The Word, 16—"Let the word of CHRIST dwell in you richly". I should think the idea here is that of a rich man coming to live in a house who, by reason of the financial resources at his command, is in a position to change completely the appearance and appointments of the place, while the previous occupant, being poor, was able to do very little toward the proper upkeep of the house. Has "the word of CHRIST" but a poor place in our hearts, or are we rejoicing in its riches? The point here, however, is not merely the heart, but also the home itself. Is the Word the test and the talisman of the dwelling? If so, two things especially are likely to ensue. (*a*) "Wisdom"— in the family conduct, plans, and relationships. (*b*) "Singing"—for this is a happy home, when the Word is the yard-stick of all behaviour. "Singing with grace" doesn't mean with gracefulness, or tunefulness, since not all of us can manage that, some even being tone deaf. The Greek has a definite article here, "the" grace, the grace of GOD— "singing with the grace in your hearts"; this, if we are Christians, we can all manage, even with gusto. "To the Lord"—if nobody else enjoys your solo, GOD will, who made the crows as well as the nightingales. That was a godly thing which, at one time, became almost a Sabbath evening institution, when the family gathered round the piano, and made the walls ring with their "psalms, and hymns, and spiritual songs". With the Word in residence as the Rich One, the melody of heart and home is assured. Let us, then, not merely read, but study, and ponder, and practise the Scriptures, that we may not simply have a poor knowledge thereof, but become increasingly possessed of its abounding wealth.

The Name, 17—"Do all in the Name of the Lord JESUS". That little word "all" is large in content—*multum in parvo,* as the Latins say. The verse also offers the bigger word, "whatsoever"—an indiarubber word, that can be stretched to include everything that life demands of us: the hard things, the humdrum things, the happy things, the homely things, the holy things—"all", "whatsoever". Herein "the Name" is to be our guiding star. (*a*) Our reason is in the Name—we "do", because He did in the home at Nazareth. (*b*) Our example is in the Name—wh left us "an example that ye should follow His steps", Peter ii. 21. (*c*) Our guidance is in the Name—as was said at the homely wedding scene, "whatsoever He saith unto you, do it", John ii. 5. (*d*) Our motive is in the Name—for "the love of CHRIST constraineth us", 2 Corinthians v. 14. When all is said and done, the Name just means Him.

These, then, are three great secrets why this that Paul envisages is no ordinary home, but the Ideal Home, exhibited here for our pleasure, and our pattern.

> "Care and doubting, gloom and sorrow,
> Fear and shame are mine no more;
> Faith knows naught of dark tomorrow,
> For my Saviour goes before:
>   Full salvation!
> Full and free for evermore!"

HIS TALK OF TONGUES

Talk of Tongues

2 Continue in prayer, and watch in the same with thanksgiving;

3 Withal praying also for us, that God would open unto us a door of utterance, to speak the mystery of Christ, for which I am also in bonds:

4 That I may make it manifest, as I ought to speak.

5 Walk in wisdom toward them that are without, redeeming the time.

6 Let your speech *be* alway with grace, seasoned with salt, that ye may know how ye ought to answer every man.

HIS TALK OF TONGUES

IV. 2–6

WHAT a lot of time we spend—and sometimes waste—in talking. So we may be quite sure that the ever-practical Paul will take up the matter, and deal with the various aspects of it from the Christian point of view.

THERE IS THE SPEECH OF PRAYER

"Continue in prayer, and watch in the same with thanksgiving," 2. (a) *"Prayer"*—what a man of prayer he was himself, and how constantly we find him longing for the prayers of others. He knows how much we Christians can do for one another if we can only pray: we could do nothing better for a man. He reckoned it as one of the pieces of a Christian soldier's armour—"Praying always", Ephesians vi. 18. I suggest that the list of armour does not end with verse 17. We understand that Paul's military guard was with him, Acts xxviii. 16; and as he picked out the parts of the soldier's accoutrement, he used each bit as a spiritual illustration of the Christian warrior's equipment. It seems that one item is missing from the catalogue —what was called the "greaves", a protection for the shins and the knees. Possibly the sentry of the moment was not wearing them just then, but our writer knew that the armour was not "whole" without them, and although because of their absence at the time he does not mention them by name, he won't leave out the spiritual truth that they stand for. The knees: why, prayer, of course. He would so much appreciate the old prophet's exhortation, "confirm the feeble knees", Isaiah xxxv. 3. (b) *"Watch"*— I dare say Paul would know of the Master's coupling together of "watch and pray", Matthew xxvi. 41. (1) Watch before you pray—that you do not rush into the audience chamber of the King; or that Satan does not spoil your spirit before ever you draw near, for—

> "Satan trembles when he sees
> The weakest saint upon his knees."

(2) Watch while you pray—lest any wandering thought come in to distract you from the holy business. Arrest that thought at once, like a policeman on the watch, "bringing into captivity every thought to the obedience of CHRIST", 2 Corinthians x. 5—arrest it "in the Name" of the King. (3) Watch after you pray—looking out confidently for the answer. Remember Charlotte Elliott's reminder—

> "Watch, as if on that alone
> Hung the issue of the day;
> Pray, that help may be sent down;
> Watch and pray."

(c) "Thanksgiving"—prayer and thanksgiving are so often joined together by Paul. This is our "Thank you" to prayer's "Please". Do you feel that we are often guilty of shocking bad manners toward GOD, in that we frequently forget to thank Him for His answers to our prayers. Moreover, how thankful we must ever be that we are privileged to pray to Him at all. Let us, then, be careful to put this right. (d) "Continue"—keep at it. Satan will, of course, do his evil utmost to hinder us; and, besides, often when "the spirit indeed is willing . . . the flesh is weak", Matthew xxvi. 41. We are so tired, so lazy, so impatient, so doubtful. We recall that the Master told more than one of His parables to press home that "men ought always to pray, and not to faint", Luke xviii. 1. We are often in such a hurry that, if the answer doesn't come at once, we drop the asking. It is well for us to bear in mind that GOD always answers true prayer—sometimes He says "Yes"; sometimes He says "No"; sometimes He says "Wait". I heard the other day of a girl who said, "Mother has always taught me that 'No' is an answer". If He does say "No" to your prayer, will you remember to view it from this threefold background—first, His love wants the best for you; second, His wisdom knows the best for you; third, His power gets the best for you. Will all that not conjure up in you a readiness for His "No"? And if He, by delay, seems to say "Wait", then "continue in prayer" until in His own time, and in His own way, your petition is granted. So may we learn how to speak to GOD. We do not need, in this great matter, to be self-taught, for "the SPIRIT also helpeth our infirmities; for we know not what we should pray for as we ought, but the SPIRIT Himself maketh intercession for us", Romans viii. 26. What a joy is this, to have Someone who is able and willing to teach us the What, and the How of prevailing prayer, so that the effectual speech of supplication may be ours, James v. 16.

THERE IS THE SPEECH OF TESTIMONY

"Withal praying also for us, that GOD would open unto us a door of utterance, to speak the mystery of CHRIST, for which I am also in bonds, that I may make it manifest, as I ought to speak," 3–4.

I ought to. So says the apostle, and so should every Christian say, for if we know GOD ourselves it is incumbent upon us to tell others of Him. "The mystery of CHRIST", the secret of the saving grace and mercy of GOD toward sinners, hid through ages, but hinted at through type and prophecy, is now laid open in the appearing of the Son of GOD from heaven, and in His suffering upon the Cross. Paul now conceives it his bounden duty to "make it manifest", to speak it clear and plain to the souls of men who need Him so desperately, as dying men need Water and Bread of Life. We find a pictorial illustration of the matter in the story of the four leprous men at the gate of Samaria, in their dilemma. A "mystery" of supply is available to their need. It is brought about by GOD through the mysterious noise of armies that He caused the Syrians to hear. While the unfortunate four discuss their dire hunger, the mystery is hid; but at last the plentiful store is revealed to them. In their excitement they take their fill; but, presently, one remarks, "We do not well, this is a day of good tidings, and we hold our peace", 2 Kings vii. 9; at which they proceed at once to "make it manifest" to the besieged city. We, too, live in a gospel day: dare we hold our peace, when multitudes around us are starving for Bread? After all, "we were allowed of GOD to be put in trust with the gospel", 1 Thessalonians ii. 4—from the moment that we were, by faith in the Saviour, put in touch with it, we were put in trust with it. Surely, then, I ought to pass it on.

I want to. Paul bids his friends pray for him to have "a door of utterance" opened to him. He knows that he ought to speak, and he longs for the opportunity to come his way. A rather cheeky boy was applying for a job; and when the prospective employer asked him, "Have you a motto in life?" he replied, "Yes, sir, same as yours". "What do you mean, son?" "Saw it on the door, sir—'PUSH'." Ah, yes; but I fancy that won't do for a Christian. Too many mistakes have been made, too many lives spoilt by trying to push doors open. This very Paul seems almost to have fallen into that error, when "they assayed to go into Bithynia, but the SPIRIT suffered them not", Acts xvi. 7, and perhaps also when they "were forbidden of the HOLY GHOST to preach the Word in Asia", 6. In his fine eagerness, he was perhaps inclined to make opportunities; but Asia was a closed door. Europe was GOD's door for him, 11–12. I wonder if I am right in holding, as I do, that it is better not to try to *make* opportunities for Christian service, but of course to be eager to *take* them when they appear. Paul here, you see, prefers praying to pushing. After all, if I may dare to put it so, GOD is expert in doors—I am "He that openeth, and no man shutteth; and shutteth, and no man openeth . . . behold, I have set before thee an open door", Revelation iii. 7–8. When He shows the way in, we may expect His blessing to follow, even though there may come opposition from enemy quarters. Thus Paul is able to write of his experience at Ephesus, "A great door and effectual is opened unto me, and there are many adversaries", 1 Corinthians xvi. 9. Of course, we must want to have opportunities of speaking a word of testimony for our Lord, and be ready to see and seize them, otherwise doors will not open. If GOD knows that we really want them, He will assuredly offer them. Perhaps, then, the wise plan will be to stop rushing and pushing, and to ask Him to guide, to gird, to guard, and, if necessary, to goad.

I can't do. Forgive the clumsy phrase; but it matches up to the other two. The apostle longs to speak of the mystery, but he regrets if he can't do it, because he is "in bonds". All the same, in his heart of hearts, he knows that prayer can change chains from an opposition into an opportunity. There in his prison in Rome, if he felt for a moment that the door was chained, prayer soon slipped the chain, and the "door of utterance" flew open to him. Of himself, he can't do it, can't push the door open, his hands were chained, but prayer moved GOD's hand to open it. Indeed so. Think of the conference he had with his fellow Jews, Acts xxviii. 17. Think of the correspondence he conducted —to Philippians, Ephesians, Colossians, Philemon. His pen was the tongue of a ready speaker, *cf.* Psalm xlv. 1. Think of the converts he won—Onesimus, Philemon 10; and soldiers who became the "saints of Cæsar's household" Philippians iv. 22. But to speak more particularly, do any of us feel that we can't do this thing, this witnessing to another? Is it shyness that keeps us back; is it fear of what those others will think, or say, or do; is it dread of saying the wrong thing, or of becoming tongue-tied in our

nervousness? You are in distinguished company. Moses
felt the same—"What shall I say . . . I am slow of speech",
Exodus iii. 13; iv. 10. To which GOD replied, "I will be
with thy mouth, and teach thee what thou shalt say".
Jeremiah felt the same—"I cannot speak, for I am a child",
Jeremiah i. 6. To which GOD replied, "I have put My
words in thy mouth". And you feel the same? Not
ashamed to speak—you want to; but afraid to speak—you
can't do? And certainly you ought to. "Let the redeemed
of the Lord say so," Psalm cvii. 2. Do you love Him
enough to trust Him, and will you open your mouth, and
begin? Remember the infallible secret, "They were all
filled with the HOLY GHOST, and began to speak . . ."
Acts ii. 4: you are not concerned with "other tongues",
it's your own tongue you are bothered about. You needn't
be. Seek His infilling, and the testimony will come out-
flowing. Open your mouth, and begin. And don't forget
that, while salvation is ours as soon as "with the heart
man believeth", Full Salvation is only enjoyed when "with
the mouth confession is made", Romans x. 10. Next—

THERE IS THE SPEECH OF BEHAVIOUR

"Walk in wisdom toward them that are without, redeeming the time," 5. In the New Testament, "walk" is frequently used for the life: the kind of way in which we
behave, whether bad, as in Colossians iii. 7, "in the which
ye also walked some time", or good, as in 1 Thessalonians
ii. 12, walk worthy of GOD, who hath called you unto His
kingdom and glory". Sometimes, alas, a Christian's walk is
not consistent with his profession. It was to one such that
the remark was made, when he was speaking of spiritual
things to an unbeliever, "Excuse me, but what you are
speaks so loudly that I cannot hear what you say". How
that man needed to heed the exhortation at the head of
this paragraph. But, wait a moment: do we not all need
it? Are we blameless in this regard? May we all so closely

"walk with GOD", Genesis v. 22; vi. 9, that such a rebuke may never be brought against us.

"*Walk in wisdom*"—says our verse. What need we have of that, if we are to display the right character, if we are to say the right word, if we are to recognise the right time, if we are to employ the right tact, which shall not put them off, but pull them in. What a comfort to know that, as well as a whole lot of other fundamental necessities, "CHRIST JESUS is made unto us wisdom", 1 Corinthians i. 30. Let us watch how He walked, and then "follow His steps", 1 Peter ii. 21. Yes, our walk talks. Do you know that strange little word in Proverbs vi. 13, "He speaketh with his feet"? A small boy was told not to walk across a certain muddy field. When he came home his mother asked him, "Did you go over the field?" "No, mum, you told me not to." She merely pointed to his shoes, covered with mud. "He speaketh with his feet." His walk was inconsistent with his profession—his lips told a lie, his feet told the truth: the other way round from the more usual inconsistency. You will know that in early days the Christian religion was dubbed "the Way", Acts ix. 2; xix. 23; xxiv. 14. How appropriate and significant a name for the following of Him who said "I *am* the Way". To company with Him is wisdom indeed.

"*Toward them that are without.*" Those that are astray must always be a concern to those who are within the fold. By all means at our disposal we must seek to win them, to lure them within. I expect you remember our Lord's parable of the Great Supper. Some of those invited refused to come, and the servants were sent out to the streets and lanes of the city, and to the highways and hedges, with the invitation. So are we bidden to the gospel feast of the Christian life, where "all things are now ready". Some do not want it; and still, in this gospel age, the invitation runs, for "still there is room". Once more, the servants of the Master are graciously commissioned to "Go

out . . . and compel [lovingly persuade] them to come in",
Luke xiv. 23. Are we intent upon that blessed task? If so,
one of our secrets must be to "walk in wisdom toward
them that are without". To that end, how often our walk
is more persuasive, and more productive, than our talk.
Both, please, as opportunity serves; but we will be specially
mindful of our behaviour, lest, by any inconsistency, we
put a stumbling block in the way of others. Some who
have been "near to the kingdom" have been put off in this
very way. It behoves us all to be very careful to seek
"wisdom" from our Lord, that we may avoid being the
cause of any such tragedy. "Make straight paths for your
feet, lest that which is lame be turned out of the way,"
Hebrews xii. 13. Pray for them, yes, indeed; but let the
life correspond. As John Keble hymns it—

> "And help us, this and every day,
>   To live more nearly as we pray."

"*Redeeming the time*"—buying up the opportunity, as
this phrase is often rendered. Losing no chance that may
present itself to "catch men" in the gospel net, Luke v. 10.
But, "redeeming", buying—such words surely contain an
idea of cost; and, assuredly, this business of soul-winning
is a costly affair. Watchfulness, patience, courage, tact,
prayer, testimony, life, energy—all this spiritual currency
builds up into the human side of the purchase cost of this
fishing industry. Recall the impelling lines of Horatius
Bonar's hymn, as he originally wrote it, not as in the
emasculated words of modern hymn books—

> "Speed, speed thy work; cast sloth away,
>   With great strong wrestlings souls are won."

May GOD lay upon us all the burden of souls, and, in the
light of His suffering, make us willing to pay the price!
Then—

THERE IS THE SPEECH OF CONVERSATION

"Let your speech be alway with grace, seasoned with salt," 6. Some years ago, Chinese Christians engaged in a form of witness which they called "gossiping the gospel" —just talking quite naturally about CHRIST and His things in the way of ordinary conversation. A very commendable form of speech for GOD, don't you think?

"*Speech.*" James iii warns us of the ill that our tongues can bring into other lives, yet how great the blessings they can bring. That is a remarkable claim made by the ungodly, in Psalm xii. 4, "Our lips are our own, who is lord over us?" No Christian can say that. CHRIST is Lord over us, our lips are not our own—nothing of ours is ours. "Ye are not your own," 1 Corinthians vi. 19. Mind, and mouth, and members belong to Him who bought us. May our lips, then, be used always for good, and for GOD. We do not forget that GOD hears what we say. Sometimes it is what distresses Him, "He hath heard your murmurings", Exodus xvi. 9. Sometimes it is what delights Him, "Then they that feared the Lord spake often one to another, and the Lord hearkened and heard it, and a book of remembrance was written before Him for them that feared the Lord, and that thought upon His Name", Malachi iii. 16. That "hearkened" is noteworthy, as if to indicate, speaking humanly, that He not only heard, but, as it were, cupped His ear to catch it all. In the first case, He had to listen; in the second case, He wanted to listen. Let us then, sometimes, as opportunity affords, engage our tongues, to believers or to unbelievers, to talk tactfully about the One who means everything to us.

"*Salt.*" Pungency sometimes, yes, when dealing with corrupt things. But graciousness always, as characterised the Master's conversation—"Never man spake like this Man", John vii. 46. If we be "in CHRIST", if He be in us, may we not catch something of His tone and accent?

Would not this mean no repetition of slander, no suspicion of uncleanness, no temper, no criticism of others, no giving as much as we get, no undue exaggeration, no even slight variation from the truth, no unkind word. Verily, "if any man offend not in word, the same is a perfect man", James iii. 2—that is, a man of full stature in CHRIST. Even as I wrote the "no's" just above, my heart turned to the old prayer, "Set a watch, O Lord, before my mouth; keep the door of my lips", Psalm cxli. 3. I think that our passage has one more thing to say about the Christian ministry of the tongue.

THERE IS THE SPEECH OF EXPOSITION

"That ye may know how ye ought to answer every man," 6. We link this up with a later passage, "Be ready always to give an answer to every man that asketh you a reason of the hope that is in you, with meekness and fear", 1 Peter iii. 15. The latter part of this verse corresponds to the "how" of our Colossian verse. When we are trying to explain to another the reasonableness of our belief, there is a proper way to do it, a true Christian spirit in which to talk. Almost as important as knowing what to say is to "know how" to say it. Like our ordinary conversation, this also is to be "alway with grace, seasoned with salt". At the very beginnings of the Christian Church we are told of two great characteristics of the apostles' "witness"—which should qualify both our public and our private testimony —"great power . . . and great grace", Acts iv. 33. Shall we not ask for strength of conviction, and sweetness of manner? Well now, if our "answer", our "reason", is to be intelligent, and in any degree effective, it will need careful and constant study. Shall we make it our aim to get a firm grasp of the meaning and teaching of the Creed and church doctrine? A useful compendium, which any average mind could thoroughly enjoy, is *The Catholic Faith* by the late Dr. Griffith Thomas, published by the Church Book

Room Press, 7 Wine Office Court, Fleet Street, E.C.4. A stiffer book, but excellent, is T. C. Hammond's *In Understanding be Men*. A splendid smaller book is the late Dr. Rendle Short's *Why Believe?* The two last are published by the Inter-Varsity Fellowship, 30 Bedford Square, W.C.1. Such books will greatly fore-arm us, if we get a real grip of them, for the giving of our "answer" to the challenge that may come to us. But, of course, our chief manual will be the Bible. To get a growing, and deepening, knowledge of it will surely be the ambition of us all. If it is to be to us, among many other things, "the Sword of the SPIRIT", Ephesians vi. 17, we must learn to wield it effectively by constant sword drill. That will come, not by reading a few verses in the morning—though that is an excellent preparation for the day—but by earnest and diligent study of the Sacred Record of GOD's dealings, and purposes of love for men. And then, added to all this equipment for the head must be a personal heart experience of GOD. This will bring the "grace" into our "answer"— not only the Book knowledge, but the Look acquaintance of Isaiah xlv. 22.

HIS ENCLOSED GROUP PHOTOGRAPH

Group Photograph

7 All my state shall Tychicus declare unto you, *who is* a beloved brother, and a faithful minister and fellowservant in the Lord:

8 Whom I have sent unto you for the same purpose, that he might know your estate, and comfort your hearts;

9 With Onesimus, a faithful and beloved brother, who is *one* of you. They shall make known unto you all things which *are done* here.

10 Aristarchus my fellow prisoner saluteth you, and Marcus, sister's son to Barnabas, (touching whom ye received commandments: if he come unto you, receive him;)

11 And Jesus, which is called Justus, who are of the circumcision. These only *are my* fellowworkers unto the kingdom of God, which have been a comfort unto me.

12 Epaphras, who is *one* of you, a servant of Christ, saluteth you, always labouring fervently for you in prayers, that ye may stand perfect and complete in all the will of God.

13 For I bear him record, that he hath a great zeal for you, and them *that are* in Laodicea, and them in Hierapolis.

14 Luke, the beloved physician, and Demas, greet you.

HIS ENCLOSED GROUP PHOTOGRAPH

IV. 7–14

I DARE say you have had the experience of receiving a letter from a friend, in which he has enclosed a group photograph of friends well-known to you both. Paul seems to have done here, in words, something of the same kind. He has grouped together, in thumbnail sketches, a number of people who are roundabout him in Rome, and who are all well-known to the church members in Colossæ. How interested they will be in these glimpses, on that Sabbath morning, in the Assembly, of their far-off comrades in the Faith, brought so vividly to sight and memory by these spoken miniatures. I dare say that we, too, may gain interest and inspiration from a study of their features, for each has a characteristic profile of his own. Take a good look at them, there in the group, one by one.

TYCHICUS—*the Man with a Message*

That word "minister" seems to denote that he was acting as a sort of personal servant to the apostle, a kind of valet, a reliable person ready at hand to do any job, to run any errand for him. A servant of his master; and, at the same time, a "fellow-servant" of the Master—the two Greek words are different. In the New Testament original, there are no less than eight different words for the idea of service.

(1) Diakonos, the ministering servant. (2) The household servant, oiketēs. (3) The subordinate servant, uperetēs. (4) The confidential servant, therapōn. (5) The public servant, leitourgos. (6) The temple servant, latreuō. (7) The responsible servant, oikonomos. And, most frequent of all, (8) The bond servant, doulos. It is the first and last of these words that are used here of Tychicus. He is not the

123

slave of Paul, he is the diakonos, the ministering servant;
but he is the sundoulos, the fellow-slave, with Paul "in the
Lord". The inspired New Testament is so exact in its use
of words.

It is often said that "no man is a hero to his own valet":
but I fancy we have an exception in this man. Paul thought
highly of him, and I suspect that he thought much of his
master. Paul certainly trusted him implicitly, and now that
this important letter has to be delivered to Colossæ, he
chose Tychicus to be his postman. I should imagine that he
was in no sense a significant-looking man; but you would
be wrong if you passed him on the road thinking him as
of no importance—he was a man with a message. He
carried this Epistle, a part of the very Word of GOD. We
also, if we are Christians, bear in our person the message
of CHRIST. Paul goes further when he says, in 2 Corinthians
iii. 3, "Ye are manifestly declared to be the epistle of
CHRIST . . . written not with ink, but with the SPIRIT of the
living GOD."

Here, then, is this insignificant man charged with such
a significant errand. But how often GOD works that way.
"Not many wise men are called, not many mighty, not
many noble," 1 Corinthians i. 26—he doesn't say not any,
but not many. "GOD hath chosen" insignificant folk. Not
that He could not have the Somebodies; but He quite
deliberately often chooses the Nobodies—a boot-maker's
errand-boy, D. L. Moody; a mill-girl, Mary Slessor. It
looks as if there's hope of a chance for you and me in
the Great Employ.

ONESIMUS—*the Man with a Past*

I wonder what the Colossian church folk thought when
they found this fellow in the Group. He belonged to that
town; had been a slave in the service of a well-to-do
member of the community there, Philemon. He had robbed
his master, and bolted. Like many another runaway thief,

or other criminal, he had found his way to the Imperial City, magnificent in its splendour, but squalid beyond words in the pestiferous purlieus behind the imposing façade. Bishop Lightfoot called it "the common sink of all the worst vices of humanity". It was to the slums of this Rome that Onesimus had gravitated. But the sovereign grace of GOD was after this sinner; and someone found him, who brought him to Paul, who brought him to CHRIST. "My son Onesimus, whom I have begotten in my bonds," Philemon 10. And now "a faithful and beloved brother who is one of us", Colossians iv. 9.

All that past is now forgiven, as, bless GOD, any man's past may be, however wicked. Paul is a true and faithful pastor; and he knows that if this man is to grow in grace, and have the joy of full salvation, he must, now that he is at peace with GOD, go and put things right with the one he has wronged. Be it borne in mind that restitution is a first principle of the spiritual life. "If thou bring thy gift to the altar, and there rememberest that thy brother hath ought against thee, leave there thy gift before the altar, and go thy way; first be reconciled to thy brother, and then come and offer thy gift," Matthew v. 23–4. Any reparation that is in our power to make must be undertaken. This is going to be a most difficult thing for Onesimus, for his erst-while employer, under the Law of the time, has powers of severest punishment. It turns out that this Philemon is another of Paul's converts—"thou owest unto me even thine own self", Philemon 19; and so the apostle writes him the personal letter, beseeching his favour for his returned slave. It is a beautiful letter, which will surely melt the heart of the recipient, and secure the boon of mercy for the rene-gade. Onesimus is to take it, and present it personally. But what if, on nearing his destination, he should get scared, and turn back? Why, Tychicus also is going to Colossæ, with the public letter to the church. Good idea, they shall travel together; and if there shall be any sign of panic,

Tychicus will deal with the matter, and keep the fearful
one up to his duty. Ay, Paul was ever a strategist!

ARISTARCHUS—*the Man with a Heart*

What a "comfort" (11) this man was to the apostle. The
first mention of him is in Acts xix. 29, where we find him
alongside of Paul in the fierce riot at Ephesus, stirred up
by the devotees of Diana. Paul escaped; but they "caught"
Aristarchus. We move on to Acts xxvii. 2, and we discover
this man still with the apostle amid the hurricane rigours
of the "tempestuous Euroclydon". Such sharing of stormy
experiences must have drawn the two very close together.
And now here he is yet, described as "my fellow-prisoner"
—sharing again; this time, some form of voluntary con-
finement.

This friend of the evangelist had learned and practised
the Christian exhortation, "Bear ye one another's burdens,
and so fulfil the law of CHRIST", Galatians vi. 2. Ultimately,
of course, "every man shall bear his own burden" (verse 5);
but, with the shoulder of our sympathy, and practical aid,
we can help to take some of the weight of the trouble off
our friend's back, even if it is only to remind them to "cast
thy burden upon the Lord", Psalm lv. 22. I have known
Christian people who have had no distinction in the exercise of public gifts; they could not lead a meeting, or give
an address, they were not on the church council, nor had
any prominent place in their church; but yet they were the
most beloved and most effective of members. They were
burden-bearers. Somehow, whenever anyone was in trouble,
it was to these folk that they went, and always found comfort and help. It is a great thing to be of the family of
Aristarchus.

MARCUS—*the Man with a Future*

But surely he, too, was a man with a past? Yes, indeed.
How happily and enthusiastically he started out on that first

missionary tour, when he went with Barnabas and Saul, as the junior member of the party, Acts xiii. 2, 5. They had a great time on the island; but when plans were being made to go on back to the mainland, Mark, for some evidently unjustifiable reason, decided that he would "depart" home, and so deserted them. After some time Paul suggested to Barnabas that they should make a return visit to the places of their previous tour with the Gospel, to exhort the converts to continue stedfast in the faith. Barnabas, dear man, was all for it; but there was strong disagreement as to whether or not they should take Mark again. Paul said "No", and of course he was right. How could they urge the young Christians to be loyally stedfast, if they took with them a young man who had deserted. Barnabas said "Yes", and of course he was right in taking Mark with him back to Cyprus, where he had not deserted. So, out of the "dissension" arose two missionary societies, instead of one.

Yes, he had a past; but that is now all over. Largely, I suppose, he had a second chance through the kindly action of his uncle. Do you think that GOD ever judges a man on a first chance? I recollect how Peter, after his dismal failure, was graciously re-instated in his apostleship to "feed" the flock. I recall how Jonah ran away from GOD, rather than go to preach to the despised Gentiles, and how "the word of the Lord came unto Jonah the second time", Jonah iii. 1. And now, here is young Mark—such a disappointment, but GOD will not leave him there. A past, yes; but as we look at him there in the group, it is his future—of which, at the moment, he is wholly unaware—that strikes us. Listen: this is the man upon whom GOD has His hand for the writing of the Second Gospel. You and I are not given the honour of *writing* a gospel, but we are privileged in *being* a gospel—

> "You are writing a gospel, a chapter each day,
>   By all that you do, and all that you say.
> Men read what you write, whether faithless, or true.
>   Say! What is the Gospel according to you?"

So John Mark gets his second chance; and he is now back again with his old leader, and Paul rejoices to have him in the group of his now faithful friends. That is a wonderful testimony that the apostle gives, when writing from his last, and more rigorous, imprisonment—"Take Mark, and bring him with thee, for he is profitable to me for the ministry", 2 Timothy iv. 11. What a glorious come-back! If any of us have wandered, let us take heed and heart, in the knowledge that, if there is sincere repentance, there remains for us a future of boon and blessedness. I don't know what, but something, for Him and His glory.

It is a poignant remark that Paul adds here—"touching whom ye received commandments: if he come unto you, receive him", 10. I suppose they heard about his early disloyalty to their friend; and if he dared to come near them, they would show him what they thought of him! No, no, says Paul, not a cold shoulder, but a warm hand. That's the way to welcome home a backslider. Look at Galatians vi. 1—"If a man be overtaken in a fault, ye which are spiritual, restore such an one in the spirit of meekness, considering thyself, lest thou also be tempted". We can happily leave the matter there.

JESUS JUSTUS—the Man with a Name

We know practically nothing about this man, except that he was a Jew, and was one of those who were a "comfort" to the apostle. We do know his name: but, what a Name! It was a quite common name in Palestine. According to the Early Church historian, Origen, it was even the name of Barabbas. "Barabbas" was only his description—"Bar", son of: "Abbas", the Rabbi. Son of the Manse, as we should say. What a pity that such a son should come to such a pass. Down the years, alas, there have been not a few tragedies somewhat of the sort. How vivid, then, was Pilate's challenge—which of the two will you have: Jesus Bar-abbas, or JESUS CHRIST? This common name is common no longer since the Saviour bore it, and did so for its significance of meaning, "for He shall save His people from their sins", Matthew i. 21. The name actually means "the LORD the Saviour". Tell me, reader, is He *your* Saviour, and your Lord?

Do you recall that James ii. 7 speaks of those who blaspheme "that worthy Name by the which ye are called". It is sometimes suggested that the name "Christians" was given to believers by way of ridicule. "The disciples were called Christians first in Antioch," Acts xi. 26. "Almost thou persuadest me to be a Christian," Acts xxvi. 28— me . . . a Christian! "If any man suffer as a Christian, let him not be ashamed," 1 Peter iv. 16. I am not so sure about this suggestion. Anyhow, it is a truly honourable and worthy name, Christians—CHRIST-ones. It takes some living up to; and only CHRIST Himself can enable us to live, and be, truly Christian. It was the living Lord who wrote to certain professors of the Name, "thou hast a name that thou livest, and art dead", Revelation iii. 1. What does He say of us who really do bear the Name—are we really living it?

EPAPHRAS—*the Man with a Passion*

This was apparently the man who, on the human side, founded the church at Colossæ; and Paul records that "*he hath a great zeal for you*", 13. It is good to come across a man with real enthusiasm—be it for art, for music, for sport, for bird-watching, or what not; but how rarely we find it amongst us Christians for the Master's cause. The Lord has Himself told us, in no uncertain terms, what He feels about "luke-warm" people, Revelation iii. 15–16— tepid Christianity. What strange bedfellows these two words make! How shall we be anything other than eager, if we have any experience and understanding of the love of GOD toward us, any real grasp of the amazing grace of the crucified and risen Lord; and how shall we be other than earnest, by the transforming power in our own lives, to commend Him to others as the living Saviour, Master, and Friend of all who Trust and Obey.

Ah yes, this Epaphras had zeal enough for the welfare and well-being of his beloved congregation. Doubtless that eagerness was evidenced in the relationship existing between them and him. He would be their comfort in hard experiences, their counsellor in solving their problems, their devoted friend along the road, their trusted leader in all the church life and personal life. But now he is miles away. He has gone off to Rome to consult Paul about that Gnostic heresy that we have spoken of in an earlier Study. Removed from them by all that long distance, he can now do nothing for them, nothing to help in nurturing these Colossian "babes in CHRIST", 1 Corinthians iii. 1.

But, can he not? I thought it was said that he had a great zeal for them. Surely, such a passion will out! No untoward circumstance will quite damp down an enthusiasm like his! What can he do for them? He can still, even so far removed, do for them the greatest thing that any Christian can do for another: he can pray, and evidently he throws into this strategic ministry all that GOD-directed enthusiasm that characterises all his work for them. Listen: *"always labouring fervently for you in prayers, that ye may stand perfect and complete in all the will of* GOD", 12. "Labouring fervently", one word in the Greek, a word of which our English "agonising" is but a transliteration. There he was, on his knees, wrestling with GOD for these people. His whole heart and soul were in it, his entire surrendered being was caught up in the task. I can imagine him rising from his knees utterly spent, completely exhausted. We should have counted ourselves as being like him, if it had been said that he grew tired of praying and gave it up; but have we ever, like him, grown tired through praying? Oh, to be thus prayer-warriors: battling for souls, with what, in his *Pilgrim's Progress,* John Bunyan calls "the weapon of all prayer". Such supplication over-leaps all distances, all barriers. The friend in China can be reached via the Throne. The unfriendly neighbour can be reached via the Throne. The believers in Colossæ can be reached by Epaphras, in distant Rome, via the Throne. The good man believed that, which is why he spent so much time in it—"always" at it; which is why he spent so much energy in it—"labouring fervently". Do we believe in this tremendous ministry of intercession? It should be a Christian's natural employ, for listen: "unto Him that loved us, and loosed us from our sins [R.V.], and hath made us . . . priests unto GOD and His Father", Revelation i. 5–6. It is the priest's particular prerogative to offer to GOD the incense of intercession. The New Testament teaches the priesthood of all believers. So let us take heed to the oft-heard challenge, "Let us Pray": let us, indeed, and that in the spirit of this dear man. I say! What attractive people the apostle has snapshotted here.

LUKE—*the Man with a Gift*

How often an affectionate relationship grows up between a man and his doctor. It seems to have been like that between Paul and his "beloved physician". It would appear that the two first met at Troas; and I would hazard the guess that Paul had there an attack of his illness, his "thorn in the flesh", 2 Corinthians xii. 7, and that he had to call in a doctor. So Dr. Luke first came into contact with his out-of-the-ordinary patient—unusual, because, as I fancy, Paul brought his physician to CHRIST. This apostle was a man of such all-round capacity, and full-orbed personality, that he was able to attract not only the lowly, like Tychicus, but the brilliantly educated, like Dr. Luke. All his own personal gifts were laid under contribution for the advancement of the Kingdom. "I am made all things to all men, that I might by all means save some," 1 Corinthians ix. 22.

What of Luke's gift? Legend has it that he was a considerable painter; but certainly he was an artist in words. What vivid and what attractive pictures he has given us, both in his Gospel, and in the Acts, in these "Stories from the Diary of a Doctor". His principal gift, of course, was that of medicine; and that gift he laid at the feet of the Divine Physician, and became the first medical missionary. It is thrilling to notice that Luke did actually join Paul's mission party from Troas onward, as we surmise from his record of the Pauline travels: note the significant change of pronouns. "*They* came down to Troas"—Luke is not with them. "*We* endeavoured to go into Macedonia," Acts xvi. 8, 10—Luke, by his use now of "we", is journeying with them. Think of Matthew's gift, keeping the accounts in his office, who, when he was converted, dedicated his pen to the Master's service, and was used for the penning of the first Gospel. And what of us? Have we some gift to use for Him—music, needlework, games, hobbies, languages, art, personality? GOD can use them each and all— yes, even Tabitha's needlework, Acts ix. 39. Most people have some gift, whether brilliant or humble. Will you let Him have your gift along with your self? You might even become known as "the beloved stamp collector"!

DEMAS—*the Man with a Bias*

This is the last man in Paul's group photograph taken in Rome. He is, to mix the metaphor, the fly in the ointment. You notice that he is the only one about whom the apostle has not one word to say. I wonder if there is any reason for that? In the private letter to Philemon he is called "my fellow-labourer", 24—but here, nothing at all. Do you think that he was already beginning to show signs of cooling off, which ended in that tragic sentence about him that Paul wrote in his very last letter—"Demas hath forsaken me, having loved this present world," 2 Timothy iv. 10. He had this fatal bias within him, though he was a Christian. We are not told what form his weakness took. John Bunyan thinks it was money—not in itself wrong, of course, but "*the love* of money is the root of all [kinds of, Gk.] evil", 1 Timothy vi. 10. You will recall the story in *Pilgrim's Progress* of how the two pilgrims, Christian and Hopeful, are accosted by a man who has discovered a silver mine, and who tries to lure them to stray out of their path, to become rich quickly. The incomparable allegorist calls that man Demas. I wonder? I do know that the temptation of riches has caused the downfall of many Christians.

Paul quite often uses the word "flesh"—and in two senses. (1) *Sometimes*, he means the component of our physical frame—"the life that I now live in the flesh", Galatians ii. 20. (2) *Sometimes*, however, he uses the word in a kind of technical sense, and the context must guide us as to its immediate connotation. In this latter connection, the "flesh" is that lower nature within, which we inherit from Adam—"the flesh lusteth against the SPIRIT", Galatians v. 17. That evil nature is the bias that we carry within our being, which will cause us to stray from the white of His holiness, and to wander off into sin. But, thank GOD, the Christian is a two-natured person, he has also within him a Divine counter-action, so that the evil warp can be controlled and conquered—"the SPIRIT [lusteth] against the flesh . . . so that ye need not do the things that ye otherwise [if left to yourself] would"—a free paraphrase of the Greek. Such a life of control by the indwelling HOLY SPIRIT is one bright aspect of Full Salvation.

Thus we close our look at the Group. The names that follow, in the close of the Epistle, are of people, not with him in Rome, as these eight are, but residing at Colossæ and neighbourhood, members of the church, to whom the apostle sends his affectionate greetings. As we conclude our contemplation of our eight, shall we not seek grace of GOD to follow their good example, and "flee . . . and follow . . . and fight", 1 Timothy vi. 11–12?

HIS KIND REGARDS

Kind Regards

15 Salute the brethren which are in Laodicea, and Nymphas, and the church which is in his house.

16 And when this epistle is read among you, cause that it be read also in the church of the Laodiceans; and that ye likewise read the *epistle* from Laodicea.

17 And say to Archippus, Take heed to the ministry which thou hast received in the Lord, that thou fulfil it.

18 The salutation by the hand of me Paul. Remember my bonds. Grace *be* with you. Amen.

HIS KIND REGARDS

IV. 15–18

IT IS a common practice, isn't it, to finish our letters with some such wishes as "My love to So and So", or "Kind remembrances to the family". Well, Paul does something of the sort here. There are certain people in the Colossian area that are known to him, to whom he sends his kind regards. I think that three words will summarise this concluding paragraph.

DEFICIENCY *is possible*

The church of the Laodiceans. It is not for nothing that Paul calls them "brethren", 15. We often use the term for our fellow Christians in a merely formal manner, with little meaning attaching to it; but in the Early Church it was a reality. The special relationship between believers is illustrated in such a passage as Galatians vi. 10, "As we have therefore opportunity, let us do good unto all men, *especially unto them who are of the household of faith*". A mutual care for members of the Family was noteworthy in those early days. "See how these Christians love one another" was the observation of lookers-on. The same words are sometimes used about us to-day, but spoken with a cynical twist. We see how, in fact, deficiency is possible within a church, a body of CHRIST, wherein "the members should have the same care one for another", 1 Corinthians xii. 25. Indeed, for the mutual relationships of all members, however different their characters, and their gifts, and their functions, it would be immensely profitable for us to study afresh that whole Corinthian chapter. The harmony of the whole is not to be disturbed by the wrongful attitude of any one member toward another. I suppose that,

137

in our bodies, the eye is the most delicate, and most important, of our outward organs; and it would appear that the hand is the most homely—but there is no reason for the former to look down disparagingly upon its more handy neighbour. "The eye cannot say to the hand, I have no need of thee"; verse 21. Neither is there to be any stupid envy or self-pity, "If the ear shall say, Because I am not the eye I am not of the body; is it therefore not of the body?" verse 16. No fancied superiority; no feelings of envy; no individual squabbles, like they had in the church at Philippi—"I beseech Euodias, and beseech Syntyche, that they be of the same mind in the Lord", Philippians iv. 2; nothing to mar the peace of the body in CHRIST. How greatly helped to this end would be these two neighbouring churches, the Colossian, and the Laodicean, by their perusal of their respective epistles (16). So far as our Epistle is concerned, being the inspired Word, no church can know real peace, real blessing, real fruit, unless it is built upon the Word of GOD.

The church which is in his house. We don't know who he was; but we do know what he was, a real believer, or he would not have thrown open his house for the assembly of GOD's people. It is interesting to note that in these days, in some of the new housing estates, when there is as yet no hall, the church meets in somebody's house—a little company forgathering here for worship. After all, the church is not the building, but the people. In the closing stages of the last war, after a bombing incident, it was said that our church in Beckenham had been destroyed. Don't you believe it. From the early hours of the next morning it was plainly evident that the church was very much alive. "Ye . . . are built up a spiritual house, an holy priesthood, to offer up spiritual sacrifices", 1 Peter ii. 5.

The church later on. This became, of course, as it grew, and developed, more organised; but, alas, not necessarily more healthy. We have only to recall the condition of the very church of the Laodiceans, that we have been thinking of, to see how gravely deterioration can set in, and deficiency become apparent. The sad record is in Revelation iii. 14–22. There was no spirit of enthusiasm— "neither cold, nor hot": tepid! There was no sense of need—"I have need of nothing": blatant self-sufficiency. There were many who had no spiritual relationship to CHRIST—"if any man . . . open the door, I will come in": they had entered in the door of the visible church, but kept closed the door to the church's Lord. What a state of church life is here revealed. It only serves to emphasize how watchful our church, and its members, should be, lest "the cares of this world, and the deceitfulness of riches, and the lusts of other things entering in, choke the word, and it becometh unfruitful", Mark iv. 19.

EFFICIENCY *is required*

"*Take heed to the ministry*", 17. This is, as you see, a special, personal message to Archippus. I wonder who he was. Perhaps he was taking the place of Epaphras—*inter regnum,* as we should say—while the latter was away in Rome, consulting with Paul. Our apostle would have him be careful to fulfil the obligation, and the responsibilities, which would now, in the absence of his leader, devolve upon him. We stay to ask whether any kind of ministry has been laid upon us. Archippus, as we suppose, acted and spoke in Epaphras' stead. Paul has something of that when he says, in 2 Corinthians v. 20, "Now then we are ambassadors for CHRIST, as though GOD did beseech you by us: we pray you in CHRIST's stead, be ye reconciled to GOD". A ministry of song; a ministry of healing; a ministry of comfort; a ministry of prayer; a ministry of testimony; a ministry of preaching; a ministry of household duty; a ministry of holy living—what, do you surmise, is your appointed ministry? Let us "take heed" to it, and see that, by GOD's grace, we use it to the help of others, and to the glory of GOD. How wonderful if we could say, "And they glorified GOD in me", Galatians i. 24.

"*Which thou hast received.*" It was not following upon his own initiative. GOD gave it to him, GOD sent him forth to do it. What strength that imparts to a man's call and commission, since if He sends, He must be held responsible for supplies. "Come now, therefore, and I will send thee," Exodus iii. 10—and to the reluctant Moses He gives the twofold assurance, "I will be with thee", Exodus iii. 12; "I will be with thy mouth", Exodus iv. 12. Again, "Go in this thy might . . . have not I sent thee?" Judges vi. 14— and the hesitant Gideon goes forth in reliance upon GOD's provision. "He Who bids you onward go, will not fail the way to show."

"*In the Lord.*" We must first be "in" Him before we can work "for" Him. Every real Christian is, by His mercy, in Him, as we have reminded each other in an earlier study. Are we then working for Him, in our several ministries, as instanced above? Paul has another proposition, which he uses to enhearten the worker: the word "with"—"we are labourers together with GOD", 1 Corinthians iii. 9. What a difference the little word makes. How much better a gardener works when his master works with him. Let the servant of CHRIST covet to have the Master working alongside, providing incentive, encouragement, and wherewithal. So—

SUFFICIENCY *is guaranteed*

The apostle has now signed the letter—rather clumsily, on account of his "bonds" by the wrist to his military guard. See our first Study. One word remains, to round off his Kind Regards—a word that, as a matter of fact, holds the secret spring of all hope of Full Salvation—"*Grace* be with you". Almost all of Paul's letters begin and end with it—Romans just ends with it. Is Hebrews by him? Anyhow, it bears his ending, this "Grace".

GOD's grace, which signifies His attitude, and His aid, is a constant wonder and theme of the apostle. Both aspects of it are vividly presented in this—"By the grace of GOD I am what I am; and His grace which was bestowed upon me was not in vain, but I laboured more abundantly than they all. Yet not I, but the grace of GOD which was with me," 1 Corinthians xv. 10.

We find that Peter joins Paul in magnifying the grace of GOD. There is an interesting Greek word, poikdos, which occurs several times in the New Testament, and which Peter uses twice, both in his First Epistle, and which A.V. translates "manifold": (a) "Ye are in heaviness, through manifold temptations," i. 6. (b) "Good stewards of the manifold grace of GOD," iv. 10. Put those two things together. On the one hand, let the five digits, all so different in character, from the thumb to the little finger, stand for the "manifold" trials and testings of life. On the other hand, let the five digits stand for the "manifold" grace. Now put the right hand over the left, and observe how the fingers of the "grace" hand exactly correspond to those of the "temptations" hand. Only an illustration; but an illustration of a beautiful fact—that whatever may be the need, there is at hand just the very grace to meet it. So these two grand apostles, so deeply acquainted with the hazards of life, join together in bearing testimony, out of their own wide and deep experience, to the all-sufficiency of this boon of GOD, available for all emergencies. As GOD Himself said to Paul, at a time when he was in distress, on account of his "thorn in the flesh"—"My grace is sufficient for thee", 2 Corinthians xii. 9. Our Epistle suggests many situations in which that provision for our "manifold" needs may be tested. Take out one or two, at random.

To make progress in the Christian life. "As ye have therefore received CHRIST JESUS the Lord, so walk ye in Him," ii. 6. We all recognise that this is essential to the healthiness, and happiness, and, indeed, the helpfulness of the Christian life. Probably, we shall all, whether in greater or less degree, desire to grow. Our problem is not What, but How? The answer is, Grace: GOD's supply for man's situation—by faith and obedience, keep clear and clean the pipe line, that the oil of grace may flow into our need uninterruptedly. "Grow in grace," 2 Peter iii. 18.

To stand up successfully to false teachings. "Beware lest any man spoil you. . . . Let no man beguile you," ii. 8, 18. Just as in our day, so in Paul's day, "the faith which was once delivered unto the saints", Jude 3, was constantly assailed with intellectual problems, as well as moral perils. We shall not be afraid to think out our theological, and spiritual, position, but we shall be assiduously on our guard against the "vain" vapourings of untruth. In other words, we shall be wise to seek the grace of diligence in the study of the Word—"Study to shew thyself approved unto GOD, a workman that needeth not to be ashamed, rightly dividing the Word of truth", 2 Timothy ii. 15. Through the Word of Holy Scripture, the HOLY SPIRIT will "guide you into all truth", John xvi. 13. So shall there be given to us the Grace of Smell. Does that phrase surprise you? But remember that when Paul is illustrating the various gifts of the Body of CHRIST's Church, he indicates the necessity of this function of spiritual quality—"where were the smelling?" 1 Corinthians xii. 17. In view of the prevalence of false teaching, it is a good thing to have what a friend of mine calls "a spiritual sense of smell"—to be so instructed in the Word as to be able, almost instinctively, to detect the false. We dealt with this in our third Study. Do you know that bit in Isaiah xi. 3, "And shall make him of quick understanding"? In the margin of that verse it says that the Hebrew word translated understanding really means scent, or smell, so that the One referred to shall be made by the SPIRIT a Person of keen scent, quickly discerning between the false and the true. This, too, is a gift of Grace.

To be the best in all home relationships. "Wives, hus-

bands; children, fathers; servants, masters," iii. 18–iv. 1.
Happy the household where there is mutual understanding
and co-operation—each for all, all for each. "Whether
one member suffer, all the members suffer with it; or one
member be honoured, all the members rejoice with it,"
1 Corinthians xii. 26. Because the rest of the family know
us so well, and because we are there often off our guard,
home is often the hardest place in which to witness, and
shine, for our Lord. But here again grace comes to our
assistance—GOD's aid for the godly. Is it fair to say that
the Saviour spent thirty years in the home training for three
years in the ministry? Was it not the observation and experience of His way in the home that enabled Mary to say
with such confidence to others in their problem, "Whatever
He saith unto you, do it", John ii. 5? Yes, home is a great
testing place, and a fine training ground—to pass the test, and
to profit from the training calls for the daily Grace of GOD.

To give Him the first place in everything. "That in all
things He might have the pre-eminence," i. 18. What a
picture and promise of the life of Full Salvation. With
Him in the first place, all else will fall into its right place.
In the far-off days, when the ladies wore long gloves on
going to a party, a small girl was struggling with the in-
scrutable problem of where to put the unending series of
buttons, when her mother explained, "It's really simple. Get
the top one in the top button-hole, and all the others will
follow right, to the last one". That truly is the case in the
spiritual life: give Him the first place, and all will follow
right. But, of course, the trouble is that wretched thing
Self. How subtly it enters even into our spiritual service:
why are we so busy in the work? Is it with a single eye
to GOD's glory, or does there enter into it any vestige of
unworthy motive, any seeking after our own glory? Let
us constantly beware even "the little foxes that spoil the
vines, for our vines have tender grapes", Song of Solomon
ii. 15. Self-control is of great importance, if He is to have

the pre-eminence; but even this control is a gift of Grace, for we are not left to exercise it by our strong will and determination, for "the fruit of the SPIRIT is . . . self-control", Galatians v. 23, R.V., margin. It is He, not we, to do it, if only we will look to Him for it. So it shall be "Not I, but CHRIST", Galatians ii. 20, which is the very essence of Grace's accomplishment in us of Full Salvation.

To continue true, without backsliding. Our eyes stray back to the group photograph, to the figure of Demas. And as we contemplate his sad decline, we recall the words of the famous old preacher, John Bradford, as he watched a poor prisoner handcuffed to a policeman, "There goes John Bradford, but for the grace of GOD". He will, if we will. Thus we have all the power of GOD Himself to keep us on the road. Let Philip Doddridge close our meditation—

> "'Twas grace that wrote my name
> In life's eternal book;
> 'Twas grace that gave me to the Lamb,
> Who all my sorrows took.
>
> Grace taught my wandering feet
> To tread the heavenly road;
> And new supplies each hour I meet
> While pressing on to GOD.
>
> Grace taught my soul to pray,
> And made my eyes o'erflow;
> 'Tis grace has kept me to this day,
> And will not let me go.
>
> Grace all the work shall crown
> Through everlasting days;
> It lays in heaven the topmost stone,
> And well deserves the praise.
>
> Oh, let that grace inspire
> My soul with strength divine!
> May all my powers to Thee aspire
> And all my days be Thine."